D1457357

# Pocket
# Menu Reader
## Spain

Ana Vázquez

**LANGENSCHEIDT**
NEW YORK · BERLIN · MUNICH · VIENNA · ZURICH

Originally published in Italy under the title of:

HOW TO EAT OUT IN SPAIN
© Gremese Editore s.r.l. – Via Virginia Agnelli
88 – 00151 Roma – Italy

English translation:
Graham Cole

Cover photo:
Mauritius, Mittenwald

© 2000 by Langenscheidt Publishers,
Inc. Maspeth, N.Y. 11378
Printed in Germany

If as we believe, cuisine is part of a country's culture, when visiting Spain it would certainly be a shame to restrict one's interest to its monuments and miss out on an aspect as important as its gastronomic tradition.

It should, however, be remembered that as a result of social, political, and cultural events, Spain did not possess what could rightly be described as a true national cuisine until the beginning of the twentieth century. However, this fact has reinforced the various culinary traditions at a local and regional level, thus avoiding the creation of a false national cuisine for the exclusive use and consumption of foreigners.

Today, every individual region of Spain offers its own local cuisine. Nevertheless, one can also talk of national cuisine, singling out characteristics, products, and ways of cooking which are common to all regions of the peninsula.

In short, being so closely connected with the habits and beliefs of its various socioeconomic classes, Spanish cuisine offers some pleasing surprises and mirrors the complexity of the country's historical events.

The visiting tourist will certainly benefit from having a good basic knowledge of the country's cuisine, as this will enable the most suitable places to be selected and prevent him or her from missing out on the chance to sample the very best dishes that the various regions have to offer. Therefore, the intention of this guide is to provide the foreign tourist with a general overview of Spanish cuisine including a description of its characteristics, typical produce and local specialties, along with indications as to the regions with the best gastronomic traditions. This volume also contains common terms and phrases and the right words for understanding and making oneself understood in the restaurant without difficulty. There is even a section offering a wide range of typical Spanish recipes to try out at home, allowing you to remember and relive the most pleasurable moments of your Spanish holiday.

## MAIN CHARACTERISTICS OF SPANISH CUISINE

In order to define the characteristics of Spanish cuisine, it needs to be remembered that there is a wide variety of gastronomic traditions which is due to several different factors. Firstly, we should remember that the country's physical geography has resulted in the natural creation of several distinct regions. For example, the peninsula is bordered by three stretches of water: the Mediterranean Sea, the Atlantic Ocean, and that wonderful fish farm, the coast of the Cantabria province. What is more, Spain has the highest summer temperatures in the whole of Europe (about 40°C, or 100° F, in Cordova and Badajoz), whilst in winter it reaches some extraordinary minimums (20°C or 25°C below zero, or 0° F, in Avila, Soria or Teruel). Finally, historical, cultural and social factors have led to the creation of regions with widely differing ways of life, habits and customs: suffice it to say that there are four official languages!
It therefore follows that the cuisines of these various regions lack common characteristics. However, from a gastronomic point of view it is possible to make a fairly precise distinction between the coastal regions, with a fish-based cuisine, and the inland areas where meat is the predominant ingredient.
Common characteristics of the whole peninsula are the

extremely frequent use of vegetables and pulses, especially in the preparation of starters, and that of spices, such as *pimentón*, red-pepper powder, that can be either mild or hot.

Pork plays an important part in Spanish cuisine and the whole animal is used, from snout to tail, especially when preparing cold cuts and meat-based dishes.

Other important ingredients are fish, shellfish and seafood, the latter being the main ingredient of the famous and highly esteemed *marisco español* that is available the whole year round.

Spain is also particularly rich in cold cuts and cold pork meats, wine and cheese, with an infinite variety available; every region, or rather every district, has its own production.

In conclusion, let us not forget the sweets, cakes and pastries with numerous specialties, usually associated with the traditions of the various religious festivals, to be found both in restaurants and pastry shops.

## THE SPANISH MENU

Before describing the classic Spanish menu, it should first be explained that it is common practice in Spain to go to the restaurant and eat *las raciones*. These are a selection of different foods that allow several products to be tasted with just one meal. This dish is extremely common and occurs in almost limitless varieties.

*Las tapas* are very popular in the Castilian regions and being a smaller-scale version of *las raciones*, are also to be found in bars. Before going home or to the restaurant, it is customary to stop off at no less than two or three bars for a glass of wine, beer or a soft drink: the aperitif is usually served with *las tapas*, delicious appetizers made up of small portions of cooked foods.

Having clarified these points, we are now ready to examine the Spanish menu. It usually consists of three courses: the "first course" that is generally rice or soup with vegetables or pulses, the "main course" that is usually meat or fish often accompanied by salad or potatoes, and a "dessert" that can be fruit, ice cream or a local sweet.

The meal will be rounded off with coffee and a local liqueur.

## SPANISH RESTAURANTS

When eating out in Spain, there is certainly no shortage of choice and at prices to suit all pockets. Nearly all the hotels have their own restaurant, and while quality may differ from one to another, the overall standard is generally more than acceptable.

In any event, however, the best way of getting to know Spanish cuisine is to go to a proper restaurant where typical local dishes are more readily available which can rightly be considered "the genuine article."

In addition to the restaurants, there are the *bodegas*, a kind of tavern, which specialize in *las raciones* and allow one to sample a bit of everything at very reasonable prices. Fortunately, we may rest assured that be it hotel, tavern, large or small restaurant, the food is never disappointing. We can add, however, that the restaurants and taverns at some distance from the main streets, and perhaps hidden away in the back streets of the old town, are well worth discovering. A good rule of thumb to finding the best area for eating out: every Spanish city has a square called "Plaza Mayor" situated in its oldest part, and it is there that the best local restaurants are to be found with the guarantee of a sumptuous, genuine cuisine.

Whilst not strictly necessary, it is advisable to book, especially on Saturdays and Sunday lunchtime.

In any event, before making a definite decision, it is well worth consulting the price list that can be found on display at the entrance to most restaurants and other eating houses. Besides offering a hint as to prices, it will also give some idea as to the type of food served.

When the bill arrives, you will usually have the opportunity of paying with one of the major credit cards, especially in cities and tourist resorts.

Prices vary according to one's chosen venue. Average cost of a full meal with drinks is around 2,500-3,000 pesetas per head. It is clear that a menu offering fresh fish will be more expensive and it is then advisable to choose somewhere in the vicinity of the port where good value for money will be offered.

Whether in bar, tavern or restaurant, the bill includes VAT or other local taxes, service and cover charge. It is customary to leave the waiter a tip in proportion to the total amount of the bill.

Typical opening hours are from noon to 3:30 P.M. for lunch and from 7.00 P.M. until late for dinner. However, many eating places are open all day.

# CHEESES

Spain boasts a wide variety of cheeses with production concentrated above all in the north of the peninsula.

The following is a description of each of the most common cheeses along with its region of origin. The list is by no means exhaustive since hundreds of different types exist. As in the case of other products, it is a good idea to seek the waiter's advice if wishing to sample the best local specialties.

**Afuega'l pitu**: Asturias. In *bable* (Asturian) dialect it literally means "drown the chick" which is due to its consistency: it is so dry that it is often eaten with honey to assist swallowing. Originally mild and white, a variety exists containing added *pimentón* which gives it a strong flavor and pink coloring.

**Alicante**: Alicante. Medium-fat cheese made with goat's milk. It is soft and white. Smells and tastes of cow's milk. It is not left to mature and should be eaten whilst fresh.

**Armada**: Castile-León. Also known as *calostro* or *sobado*, it is the only known cheese produced with cow's colostrum, from second or third milking (up to the fifth). Fat content is 44%. It is prism-shaped with rounded edges. The rind is medium hard and white without holes. The cheese itself has a medium-hard consistency. Flavor is strong and slightly bitter. Keeps for up to 3 years.

**Burgos**: Castile-León. This full-fat soft cheese is made from sheep's milk. It is not left to mature and should be eaten straight away. White and cylinder-shaped, it has a mild taste and a distinctive fragrance. Will not keep for more than 48 hours.

**Cabrales**: Asturias. A mixture of cow's, sheep's and goat's milk. The most prized variety is obtained by using the rennet of kids or lambs which have been slaughtered immediately after suckling and before the milk has been digested. The greenish color is due to a particular mold which develops whilst the cheese is left to mature in caves. The whole cheeses are covered with animal droppings as tradition requires. Once the cheese has reached the right degree of greasiness, it is wrapped in maple leaves and is then ready for sale. It has an intense smell and a fairly strong flavor.

**Cerebro**: Galicia. A half-fat cheese made from cow's milk with a mushroom shape. The rind is white and medium hard with cracks. The cheese itself is medium hard, white, and has a fairly bitter flavor. It is usually eaten fresh, but can be kept for up to six months.

**Gamonedo**: Asturias. Also known as *gamoneu*. This medium-fat cheese is similar to *cabrales* but is left to mature for a shorter period and in different conditions. This means that the mold does not have the same effect and the cheese obtained contains less fat. A further difference is that it is not wrapped in maple leaves.

**Gorbea**: Basque Country. It is obtained by using sheep's milk and has a fat content of 45%. The rind is yellow, hard and smooth. The cheese itself is slightly yellow and of firm consistency with holes. Strong smell and flavor. It is left to mature for a month and will keep for between 1 and 2 years.

**Idiazábal**: Basque Country. Other names are *urbia, aralar* and *urbasa*. A full-fat cheese made from sheep's milk, it is smoked and has a very particular smell. The rind is smooth whilst the cheese itself is yellow in color. It is left to mature for a month and will keep for one year.

**León**: Castile-León. Full-fat cheese obtained from cow's milk. It contains a great deal of salt. The cheese itself is white, medium-hard and strong-flavored.

**Orduña**: Basque Country. Full-fat cheese obtained from sheep's milk. It has a hard, yellowish rind and a sharp flavor.

**Pasiego prensado**: Cantabria. Made from whole cow's milk, this is a soft cheese with a white, smooth crust. It is mild-tasting and smells of fresh cream. Prepared in only a few days, it can be kept for months.

**Pasiego sin prensar**: Cantabria. It is a full-fat cheese made from whole cow's milk, although sheep's milk is sometimes added. The cheese itself is soft with a mildish flavor and the smell of milk. It is a fresh cheese which will keep for no more than a week.

**Picón de Treviso**: Cantabria. A full-fat cheese which is very similar to *cabrales*. Usually made from whole cow's milk, although goat's and sheep's milk are sometimes used. The rind is gray and is covered with the leaves of several different trees. The cheese itself is medium hard and has a yellowish-white and blue coloring. Intense aroma and very sharp flavor. It is left to mature for 6 months.

**Puzol**: Valencia. Full-fat cheese made from sheep's milk. It is soft, white and rindless. It is not left to mature and should be consumed within 24 to 48 hours.

**Queso de los Beyos**: Asturias. Also known as *beyusco*, it is a hard cheese made from sheep's or goat's milk, or sometimes both. In recent years the tendency to use cow's milk has developed. It is a full-fat, mature, slightly-smoked cheese.

**Quesucos de Lebeña**: Cantabria. It is also called *quesines* or *quesucos de Avila*. It is a medium-hard, smoked cheese made from cow's, goat's and sheep's milk (or sometimes just cow's milk). Fat content is fairly high. The cheese itself has a firm consistency, yellowish color and a distinctive smell. Will keep for only a short time.

**San Simón**: Galicia. It is prepared using whole cow's milk and has a fat content of 26%. It is pear-shaped. The rind is smoked, hard and white. The cheese itself has a firm consistency and is creamy with a slightly bitter taste. It is left to mature for a month and will keep for up to 2 years.

**Soria**: Castile-León. Full-fat, fresh cheese made from goat's milk. It is white with a salty flavor.

**Tetilla**: Galicia. It is prepared using whole cow's milk and has a fat content of 40%. It is white, pie-shaped and rindless. It has a distinctive smell and a very pleasant taste that is slightly salty and bitter.

**Ulloa**: Galicia. Also known as *gallego*, *patela* and *perilla*. It is made from cow's milk and has a fat content of 45%. It is either pie-shaped or in the form of a flat cylinder. The cheese itself is soft and white, whilst the rind is yellowish with a certain elasticity.

**Valdeteja**: Castile-León. Cheese with an elevated fat content made from whole goat's milk. The rind is smooth, dry, medium hard and yellowish in color. Flavor is sharp.

**Villalón**: Castile-León. Also known as *pata de mulo*, it is made from sheep's milk. It is a fresh, full-fat cheese similar to *burgos* (see above). It is soft, white and rindless.

Cold cut meats are products typical of Spanish gastronomic culture. You will find them all over the peninsula in abundant supply and with thousands of different shapes and flavors. They can be placed into different groups according to the method of preparation and the ingredients used: a distinction can be made between smoked products (the north of Spain), those with spices (all over the Mediterranean zone), those with *pimentón* – powdered red pepper similar to paprika – and lastly those with garlic (in Andalusia and Estremadura). We should also add to this list products made from game which are commonly found all over Spain, and those from the Canary Islands that have special characteristics.

**Andoya**: Asturias. A smoked cold cut meat made using loin meats. *Xuan* is a variety containing added cow- and pig-tongue.

**Blancos**: Castile-La Mancha. Pork cold cuts prepared with lard, lean meat and bacon chopped into pieces and mixed with eggs and spices such as white and black pepper, nutmeg, etc. The presence of the eggs makes them highly perishable and for this reason they must be consumed immediately.

**Blanquet**: Balearic Islands/Catalonia/Valencia. Another pork cold cut meat made using lard, lean cuts, bacon and the head of the pig. These are mixed with white pepper, cinnamon, cloves, nutmeg, pine nuts and salt. May be eaten raw, roasted or fried.

**Botelo**: Galicia. A smoked cold cut meat, prepared from small pieces of rib, vertebra and other bones along with their muscular tissue. Added to the meat are pig's lard, garlic, the famous *pimentón* (both mild and hot varieties), and oregano. It is eaten boiled.

**Butifarra**: Catalonia/Valencia/Murcia/Balearic Islands. This cold cut meat is typical of the entire eastern zone of the peninsula. Its ingredients are lean cuts of pork, bacon and lard, and just one spice: pepper. Nevertheless, its method of preparation can vary from region to region, with the addition of other ingredients such as rice, liver, onion, etc.

**Cecina**: Castile-León. Similar to ham but prepared from the lower part of the leg of pork. There exists a variety of *cecina* which uses billy goat instead of pork.

**Chistorra**: Navarra. Classic local cold cut meat made from pork and beef with bacon and lard. Spice is provided by the ever-present *pimentón*. It can be eaten roasted, grilled or fried.

**Chorizo**: the whole of Spain. The typical Spanish salami prepared from lean cuts of pork and lard. Its characteristic red color is due to the added *pimentón*. There are an infinite number of varieties as it is produced all over the peninsula and on the islands.

**Fariñón**: Asturias. One of the main characteristics of this cold cut meat is the presence of corn meal amongst the ingredients. The others are lean pork, lard and pig's blood, whilst the spices are comprised of oregano, bay leaf and *pimentón*.

**Fuet**: Catalonia. Typical local salami whose ingredients are lean pork and rindless bacon spiced with white pepper. It is also produced using belly of spring lamb with the notable addition of sugar.

**Jamón**: the whole of Spain. This is the famous Spanish ham which like *chorizo* is produced in virtually every Spanish region.

**Lacón**: Galicia. This cold cut meat is prepared using shoulder of pork. The bone is removed and salt is added to the meat. This is certainly one of the most typical of the region of Galicia.

**Lomo embuchado**: Castile/Andalusia/Estremadura/Aragón. This cold cut meat is prepared from fatless loin of pork. Main spices used are *pimentón* and oregano. It is eaten raw.

**Longaniza**: the entire peninsula. Very similar to *chorizo* since it contains the same meat. However, the spices and tripe used differ from region to region.

**Morcilla**: the whole of Spain. The basic ingredients are always the same: lard, fat, pig's blood and above all, onion. Regional variations may result from the addition of other ingredients such as rice, sugar, egg, etc. However, it is usually cooked in the same way: boiled.

**Morcón**: Estremadura/Andalusia/Valencia. This cold cut meat is typical of the southern peninsula and its ingredients are lean cuts of pork and pig's head, salt, pepper, *pimentón* and garlic. In some areas, white wine is added. It is eaten raw.

**Salchicha**: Estremadura/Castile. Lean meat, fresh lard, white pepper, oregano and mild *pimentón* are the basic ingredients of this type of cold cut meat. The added spices are subject to variation: one may find nutmeg, cloves, garlic, cinnamon, etc.

**Salchichón**: central regions. This is almost identical to *chorizo*, the one difference being the absence of *pimentón*.

**Sobrasada**: Aragón/Alicante/Catalonia/Balearic Islands. It is made using lean pork and pig's lard with the addition of *pimentón*. Once preparation is complete, a sauce is obtained which is smooth and of equal consistency: it is eaten spread over bread.

**Torteta**: Catalonia/Aragón. This popular product is of dark appearance with a mild flavor. Its ingredients are pig's blood and cinnamon. It is usually eaten fried or roasted.

*Los mariscos* (shellfish and other seafood) are a very important part of Spanish gastronomic culture, especially in the peninsula's northern regions, since the Cantabrian coast is the main source of shellfish and other crustaceans. It is therefore fitting that an entire section be dedicated to these most excellent dishes that are normally eaten boiled or grilled without losing their natural flavor. Tradition wants that the best months for *mariscos* are those containing the letter "R"; therefore, they are best avoided in May, June, July and August.

**Almeja**: clams are one of the most popular shellfish due to their characteristic delicate flavor. From a gastronomic point of view, the methods of preparation are numerous: from simple steaming to more sophisticated recipes, without forgetting that they are also eaten raw with a sprinkling of lemon.

**Berberecho**: a shellfish with a semicircular shell, smaller than the clam but no less tasty. Can be eaten in many ways including raw, with lemon, fried, boiled, etc.

**Bígaro**: a small rock snail, it is boiled and usually eaten as a starter.

**Buey de mar**: crustacean which is the largest member of the crab family. Despite its size, it is somewhat lacking in flesh. The claws are the tastiest part, whilst liver and roe are also quite delicious.

**Cangrejo de mar:** This sea crab is one of the most popular. Its meat is quite exquisite but is difficult to extract.

**Centollo**: is the king of Spanish shellfish; a species of spider crab, it is eaten boiled with a pinch of salt and a bay leaf.

**Cigala**: the quality of this species of scampi depends on the temperature of the sea: the colder the water where it lives, the more choice is its meat.

**Chirla**: is a shellfish related to the clam but of smaller dimensions. For this reason it commands a lower price and is therefore often used as a substitute.

**Gamba**: prawns are one of the most popular shellfish of the coastal regions, especially in bars that serve the famous *tapas*. Methods of preparation include grilled, boiled, with garlic, etc.

**Langosta**: if the king of the crustaceans is the centollo, the queen has to be the lobster. The cooking point needs to be just right, not over or undercooked, in order to fully appreciate the flavor and smell of the sea: in this case its taste is really worth savoring. The tastiest, and most sought after variety is the *bogayante* that can be identified by its blue shell and larger claws.

**Langostino**: it is a species of baby lobster found in Mediterranean waters and also on the northern coast.

**Mejillón**: mussels. Known as the poor man's *el marisco*, but one could certainly say "blessed are the poor"... mussels are excellent food, having both a high nutritional value (they are very rich in proteins, calories and fats) and an exquisite flavor. Methods of preparation are numerous: boiled, steamed, with lemon, with spicy sauces, etc.

**Nécora**: is a variety of *cangrejo de mar* (see above) and some will say that it is the best seafood there is. A peculiarity of this crustacean is the fifth pair of claws which are oar-shaped. Eaten in all regions.

**Ostra**: the queen of shellfish. Whether raw or boiled, oysters are always to be found in the best restaurants, although they are most closely associated with the Christmas period. Spanish oysters are considered amongst the most delicious in the whole world.

**Percebe**: although a crustacean, the barnacle could easily be mistaken for a shellfish. It is divided into two parts: the shell and the stalk, and it is the latter part that is edible. Boiled and served immediately, it is yet another seafood delicacy that is well worth trying even though it is somewhat expensive. The smaller examples of this crustacean are the tastiest ones.

**Vieira**: these shellfish are amongst the tastiest on offer with abundant meat. This allows thousands of different dishes to be prepared, although they are also excellent eaten raw.

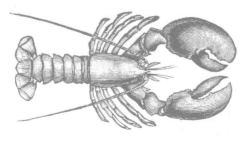

# SWEETS, CAKES AND PASTRIES

Every region of Spain has its own recipes for local homemade sweets. Many restaurants and other eating places offer delicious homemade desserts prepared to a traditional recipe.

The infinite variety of Spanish sweets makes it impossible to list them all. We therefore propose a select list of the better-known ones that you will find in restaurants and pastry shops throughout the country.

**Almendras garrapiñadas**: almonds and sugar are placed in a saucepan and heated until the sugar turns to caramel and forms a coating over the almonds.

**Arroz con leche**: a kind of risotto cooked in milk and flavored with butter, sugar, cinnamon and egg.

**Bizcochos**: small round cakes consisting of sponge cake soaked in rum.

**Brazo de gitano**: Cylindrical, like a Swiss roll, it consists of sponge cake soaked in syrup, filled with custard and covered in meringue.

**Buñuelos**: fritters of flour, eggs, sugar, butter, lemon and brandy; they are fried and covered in sugar.

**Crema catalana**; as the name suggests, it is a sweet typical of Catalonia. It consists of a cream made from sugar, milk, eggs and lemon which is then covered with a layer of caramel.

**Churros**: although these sweets are a specialty of Madrid, they are nowadays found all over the country. The mixture consisting of flour, water and salt is divided into portions vaguely resembling a tube: these are then fried and sprinkled with sugar. They are traditionally eaten on New Year's Day with a nice cup of hot chocolate.

**Ensaimada**: spiral-shaped pastry filled with cream. A typical specialty of Catalonia and the Balearic Islands, it is by now a common sight in almost every Spanish pastry shop.

**Flan**: a pudding with a thousand possible flavors including chocolate, orange, coffee, lemon, etc. It is prepared with both egg and vanilla.

**Helados**: the best Spanish ice cream is to be found above all in coastal areas, without doubt for climatic reasons. Nevertheless, it can also be found in other regions and once again in an infinite number of flavors.

**Lenguas de gato**: pastries prepared with simple ingredients – flour, eggs, sugar, butter – but with a distinctive tongue shape as suggested by the name itself, which literally means "cat's tongue".

**Manzanas al horno**: oven-baked apples with a part removed to enable orange juice, yoghurt and sultanas to be added.

**Natillas**: similar to a flan, vanilla flavored.

**Pastel de la abuela**: a kind of tart containing apricot jam.

**Polvorones**: a sweet with a slight hint of cinnamon. It is noted for the fact that it melts in the mouth. Usually eaten at Christmas.

**Tocinillos**: a kind of pudding that is very sweet and of rich consistency.

**Torrijas**: this is nothing more than slices of bread soaked in milk and then egg. They are then fried in a frying pan and finally left to cook in wine along with some sugar.

**Yemas**: sweets prepared with egg yolks. Various flavors exist including lemon, orange, etc. They are somewhat jelly-like.

Spain is a country renowned for its wines. Hundreds of
types are produced, from whites to rosés, and reds to
liqueur-like dessert wines. Every region boasts its own
special type. Castile is noted for its red wines, such as
Cava di Catalogna, whilst Andalusia is famous for Jerez.
As an entire book could be written on the subject, we
shall restrict our list to the better-known wines and their
places of origin.

**Albariño**: Galicia. A very particular white wine famous
throughout Spain. It has a bitter taste and is excellent
served with *los mariscos.*

**Alcublas**: Valencia. White wine with a slight hint of
almond. It is between 10° and 13° proof.

**Betanzos**: Castile-León. A red wine, light in both body
and color, with a bitter flavor.

**Bierzo**: Castile-León. White, red and rosé varieties exist. It
is flavored with fruit and is between 10° and 11° proof.

**Cava**: Catalonia. Many varieties exist but it is always
sparkling white and served chilled.

**Cheste**: Valencia. Dry white table wine, 15° proof.

**Chulilla**: Valencia. Red dessert wine, 13° proof.

**Haro**: Murcia. Light red wine, slightly bitter but very
refreshing.

**Jerez**: Andalusia. A typical wine of the region. There are
many types, but they are always white, quite dry wines
with a high alcoholic contert. Must be served very cold.

# WINES

**Jumilla monastrel**: Murcia. Very aromatic wine with a cherry-red color, 15° proof.

**Jumilla seco**: Murcia. Red table wine with the same alcoholic strength as the *monastrel*.

**Los Oteros**: Castile-León. Light red wine between 10° and 13° proof.

**Monterrey**: Galicia. Both red and white varieties exist. Both have a high alcoholic content and whilst not particularly bitter, neither has much of a fragrance.

**Montilla**: Andalusia. Similar to *Jerez*, but more bitter with a slight hint of almond.

**Montroy**: Valencia. Sweet Muscat dessert wine.

**Ribeiro**: Galicia. Typical local wine. It is not drunk from a wine glass, but a small kind of cup is used. It has a pleasant taste and is 13° proof.

**Rosal**: Galicia. A cheerful white wine flavored with fruit.

**Rueda**: Castile-León. A red aged wine, 15° proof.

**Toro**: Castile-León. A dark full-bodied red wine. It is flavored with fruit and has a high alcoholic content.

**Valdeorras**: Galicia. Clear dry white wine, 12° proof.

**Valdevimbre**: Castile-León. A light fragrant red wine flavored with fruit.

There are some other typical local products in Spain that do not fall into the categories previously covered, but are certainly worth trying or even buying to take back home. Once again, our list is not exhaustive and only includes the more important products.

**Canapés**: small triangular slices of bread garnished with a variety of different sauces. Commonly served in the more sumptuous restaurants as hors-d'oeuvres.

**Empanada**: it is a savory pie with puff pastry or dough that may be filled with various ingredients. The most common fillings are tuna or minced meat with tomato sauce and onion. Typical dish of the regions of Galicia and Asturias, it is now commonly found throughout the whole country.

**Empanadilla**: a kind of savory pancake that contains the same ingredients as *empanada* and is fried.

**Migas**: cubes of bread that are fried and eaten along with the traditional Spanish purée.

**Sangría**: this is one of the most famous Spanish drinks and originates from the southern central region. It is a cocktail obtained by mixing red wine, Jerez, orangeade, sugar and slices of fruit (apple, pear, orange and lemon). It is usually served chilled.

**Sidra**: Asturias. Typical of this region, it is the end result of the complete or partial fermentation of apple juice. It has a bitter taste and is 6° proof. It is drunk from a special wide glass and is poured as follows: the bottle is taken in the right hand and placed above one's head; the glass is

held in the left hand at waist height, at which point a
quantity of cider equal to 180 cc is poured. This is known
as "culin" and is drunk in one single mouthful. Everyone
drinks from the same glass.

**Torta**: a sweet flat cake covered in sugar that is to be
found in food stores and cakeshops.

**Albóndigas**: small balls of minced meat that are fried and then cooked in a thousand different ways.

**Bechamel**: creamy sauce prepared with milk, flour and butter. It is used above all for oven-cooked dishes. Pieces of chicken or veal are added to the sauce to make Spanish croquettes (very rarely are they made with potato).

**Escalopes**: breaded minute steaks.

**Filete**: any type of fried minute steak.

**Puré**: mashed potatoes served along with the meat, but also as a starter to which vegetables are added. In the latter case its consistency is a lot more liquid.

**Rollos**: roulades of meat with filling; they come in various sizes with the smaller type known as *niños envueltos*.

Even though the dishes described in this chapter have different regional origins, today they are commonly found throughout the country and are now firmly established as part of Spain's gastronomic heritage.

This does not necessarily mean that some dishes are better in their respective zones of provenance. It is worth giving them a try even when cooked to a recipe which does not follow the original to the letter.

The dishes mentioned below are listed in alphabetical order according to their Spanish name and an indication as to where you will find them on the menu.

**Alcachofas rellenas** (Stuffed artichokes): side dish. Fried artichokes with a filling of ham and bread that is also fried.

**Almejas a la marinera** (Clam marinade): starter or *ración*. A plate of clams cooked with carrot, leek, lemon, garlic, parsley and flour.

**Almejas guisadas** (Clams): starter or *ración*. A plate of clams cooked with abundant onion.

**Anguilas al horno** (Baked eel): main course. The eel is first cooked with abundant onion and then put in the oven.

**Anguilas con guisantes** (Eel and peas) main course. In this case the eel is cooked with onion, peas and *pimentón* but is not placed in the oven as baked eel. (See above).

**Arroz blanco** (White rice): starter or sometimes all-in-one dish. Boiled rice with fried tomatoes and sometimes also fried egg.

**Arroz con almejas** (Rice and clams): starter. The clams are first cooked along with onion, then added to the rice, and finally mixed together in a frying pan.

**Arroz con riñones** (Rice and kidneys): starter. Identical in all respects to the previous dish apart from the addition of kidneys.

**Atún asado** (Baked tuna): main course. The fish is cooked with abundant onion and served with a side dish of potatoes.

**Atún con tomate** (Tuna and tomato): main course. Similar to the previous dish but cooked in a tomato sauce. Sometimes bell peppers may be added.

**Bacalao al horno** (Baked dried salted cod): main course. The fish is prepared with a little tomato, parsley and white wine. There are, in fact, many other dishes which have dried salted cod as the main ingredient and these are covered in the section, "Regional Dishes." It is a commonly used fish in the restaurants of northern Spain, although it can now be found all over the country.

**Besugo al horno** (Baked sea bream): main course. The fish is baked in the oven with potatoes and onion.

**Cabrito asado** (Roast kid goat): main course. This dish is typical of the central regions of the peninsula. The meat is cooked in the oven with a few potatoes.

**Calamares a la romana** (Deep-fried squid): *ración*. Deep-fried squid rings with a sprinkling of lemon.

**Calamares en su tinta** (Squid): main course. The squid are cooked in their own black ink sauce with abundant onion and a little ham.

**Callos** (Tripe): *ración*. Famous throughout Spain, this dish is extremely spicy due to the fact that the tripe is cooked along with abundant chili pepper and *pimentón*.

**Canelones** (Cannelloni): all-in-one dish. This dish was of course imported from Italy, but is by now commonly found throughout Spain.

**Carne mechada**: main course. A cut of veal similar to that often used for pot roasts: the meat is larded (small cuts are made into which pieces of lard are inserted) although bell peppers, carrots, etc. are also added. It is cooked in its juices and then cut into thin slices for serving.

**Cocido madrileño**: all-in-one dish. Whilst its origins can be traced to Madrid, as its name would indicate, it is in fact one of the hallmarks of Spanish cuisine. It effectively consists of two courses. Firstly chick-peas, pork, salami and savoy cabbage are cooked together; the resulting broth is served with pasta, as a soup, and makes up the first course. The second course follows, consisting of the chick-peas, meat and vegetables. This is a somewhat heavy dish that is best suited to the winter months.

**Cochinillo asado**: main course. Oven-roasted suckling pig. A typical dish of the Castile region, it can now be found in many Spanish restaurants. In the local Castilian restaurants, it is cut with a plate rather than a knife in order to show how tender it is.

**Codorniz en su salsa** (Quail): main course. The quail are cooked with onion, white wine and a little flour.

**Coliflor frita** (Fried cauliflower): starter. The cauliflower is first chopped into small pieces, then boiled in salted water, and finally covered in flour and fried. Afterwards it is cooked with a little white wine and tomato.

**Compota de manzana**: dessert. Apples cooked with lemon and sugar. Pears may also be used.

**Conejo** (Rabbit): main course. The rabbit is cut into small pieces and cooked with a little onion, mushroom and white wine.

**Congrio con almejas** (Conger eel and clam): main course or all-in-one dish. Delicious. The eel is cooked in slices together with the clams, a little onion, and white wine.

**Chanfaina**: *ración*. A rather particular dish that is prepared with the parts of the pig of less common usage: heart, lung, blood, and abundant *pimentón*.

**Chipirones fritos**: main course. Small whole squid, stuffed with their own tentacles, coated in flour, and then fried until golden and crunchy.

**Chuletas/Chuletillas de cordero** (Spring-lamb cutlets): main course. The cutlets may be grilled or cooked in a frying pan and are served with a salad or French fries.

**Chuletón** (Giant steak): main course. A very large steak that can weigh more than 2 pounds (1 kilo) grilled and served with a salad or French fries.

# NATIONAL DISHES

**Embutidos mixtos**: hors-d'oeuvre. A selection of appetizers with ham, salami and different cheeses.

**Ensaladilla rusa** (Russian salad): starter. Usually eaten during the summer months, it is a mixture of potatoes, sliced carrots, peas, tuna, hard-boiled eggs, and mayonnaise.

**Entrecote de ternera**: main course. Roast veal with potatoes or vegetables.

**Espárragos** (Asparagus): *ración*. The asparagus is boiled and eaten as it is, or with a little mayonnaise.

**Filetes de ternera** (Veal minute steaks): main course. The steaks are cooked in the frying pan, usually with garlic, and are served with a salad or French fries.

**Filetes empanados** (Breaded minute steaks): main course. The minute steaks are usually served with fried peppers or potatoes.

**Gratinado de berenjenas** (Eggplant au gratin): side dish. Sliced eggplant covered in grated cheese and cooked in the oven until a light crust is formed.

**Huevos al plato** (Egg platter): main course. The eggs are served in the same casserole dish in which they are cooked along with a mixture of peas, ham and peppers.

**Jamón con guisantes** (Ham and peas): main course. Small pieces of ham and peas cooked with onion and white wine.

**Judías verdes** (French beans): starter. The beans are first boiled and then cooked with a little tomato and potatoes.

**Langostinos** (Baby lobsters): *ración*. They may be grilled or boiled. In the latter case they are served with a sprinkling of lemon.

**Lenguado al horno** (Baked sole): main course. The fish is baked in the oven and served with potatoes.

**Lubina asada** (Sea bass): main course. Oven-baked bass with pepper, lemon and parsley.

**Manzanas rellenas de nuez y coco** (dessert): after scooping out the center of the apples and removing the core, they are filled with a mixture of sugar, walnuts, and coconut and "sealed off" with butter. The apples are then sprinkled with Jerez and baked in the oven.

**Mejillones al vapor** (Steamed mussels): *ración*. The steaming brings out the full flavor of the mussels and they merely require a squeeze of lemon before serving.

**Menestra** (Soup): starter. A minestrone of mixed vegetables and small pieces of pork or veal, it is usually eaten in the winter months.

**Merluza a la cazuela** (Hake): the fish is cooked together with clams, asparagus, and peppers. It is served in the same casserole dish in which it is cooked.

**Milhojas** (Millefeuille or Napoleon): dessert. A rich confection of puff pastry split and filled with cream and meringue.

**Morcilla**: *ración*. The main ingredient is black pudding either fried or boiled; in both cases abundant *pimentón* is added. This fairly spicy dish is typically found in all Spanish regions and is well worth trying.

**Nata con nueces** (Walnuts and cream): dessert. A specialty of the Mediterranean regions. The shelled walnuts are served in a sundae dish along with the cream.

**Paella**: all-in-one dish. This is certainly the best known dish of all as regards Spanish cuisine and originates from Valencia. It is a risotto containing pork and chicken, peppers, mussels and clams, a little tomato, peas, and saffron for coloring. However, there are a thousand, local variations of this recipe. It may be prepared exclusively with meat or just fish, but in any event it is worth trying.

**Patatas con carne** (Meat and potatoes): all-in-one dish. A dish of rice, veal and potatoes. There is another recipe that uses prawns, but the main spice is always *pimentón*.

**Pato al horno** (Roast duck): main course. The duck is oven-roasted along with the potatoes.

**Pechugas de pollo** (Chicken breast): main course. The chicken breasts are first fried and then placed in a casserole dish and cooked with a few peppers, tomato and onion.

**Picadillo**: *ración*. This dish is prepared with the ingredients used for a normal salami, but instead of being stuffed into the skin, the mixture is fried.

**Pimientos rellenos**: *ración*. Dish made with stuffed bell peppers baked in the oven.

**Pincho moruno**: main course. Grilled pork kebabs, with pieces of sausage and peppers spiced with hot *pimentón*.

**Pollo asado** (Roast chicken): main course. Oven-roasted chicken and potatoes.

**Pulpo a la gallega** (Octopus): main course. The octopus is boiled with potatoes and then cut into not very large pieces. It is seasoned with a little oil and spicy *pimentón*.

**Revuelto de gambas y ajetes**: *ración*. Scrambled eggs with fried prawns and garlic.

**Rollos de tenera** (Veal roulades): main course. Classic dish of veal roulades cooked in an earthenware casserole dish with a few vegetables.

**Salmón asado** (Baked salmon): main course. The fish is cooked in the oven and served with a few potatoes or a salad.

**Sardinas fritas** (Fried sardines): *ración*. Typically found in the northern regions where it is a firm favorite amongst the local inhabitants.

**Solomillo**: main course. Sliced or whole joint of pork cooked with carrots, peppers and other vegetables.

**Sopa de ajo**: starter. A simple soup of water, bread, garlic and *pimentón*. Similar to the bread soup of certain Italian regions, it is traditionally eaten on New Year's Eve.

**Sopa de puré**: starter. A fairly liquid purée of vegetables, pulses and sometimes meat.

**Sorbete de naranja**: (Orange sherbet): dessert. Made with oranges, it is a bit like ice cream but with a less creamy consistency.

**Suflé de patatas**: main course. A timbale (or kind of flan) of potatoes with layers of vegetables and minced meat (usually veal).

**Tortilla española** (Spanish omelette): *ración* or main course. A potato and onion omelette. Very simple but quite excellent. A dish worth ordering in the restaurant or trying out at home.

**Tortilla francesa** (French omelette): main course. A plain egg omelette. If asparagus is added, the name is *tortilla de esparragos,* with cheese *tortilla de queso*, etc.

**Tortilla de ropa vieja** (Leftovers omelette): main course. Like the *tortilla española* but with the addition of the previous day's leftovers: meat, vegetables, pulses... anything goes.

**Tortilla paisana** (Country omelette): main course. Like the *tortilla española* but with added potatoes and vegetables such as zucchini, bell peppers, etc.

**Truchas al horno** (Baked trout); main course. Oven-cooked trout stuffed with ham.

**Truchas escabechadas** (Trout in vinegar): main course. Instead of using oil, the trout are marinated in vinegar.

Listing the infinite variety of regional specialties would take up far more space than we have available. In the circumstances, we shall restrict our list to the more common local dishes which are typically found in each region. As a brief introduction to this section, a description of the main characteristics of each region's cuisine is offered.

The layout is the same as for "National Dishes" with an indication as to the position of the dish on the menu along with its main ingredients.

## ANDALUSIA

Andalusian cuisine has always been considered poor, primitive and meager. The region's gastronomic tradition is restricted to just a few specialties, such as the famous *gazpacho andaluz*.

However, it should not be forgotten that in Andalusia eggs are a very important ingredient and are used in a wide variety of ways: scrambled, fried, etc. An important place is also held by the region's vegetables and small fried fish. Bull's meat is typical of the area, but veal and beef are also widely used.

Ham is a major ingredient of Andalusian cuisine.

**Abajá de Algeciras**: starter. A kind of soup consisting of fish stock with white wine. The fish is served afterwards as a second course.

**Chanfaína**: main course. Stewed chicken served in a sauce of onion, bell peppers, almonds, nutmeg.

# REGIONAL DISHES

**Gazpacho andulaz**: all-in-one dish. A cold soup of raw vegetables prepared with tomato, cucumber, bread, garlic, bell peppers, oil, salt, and vinegar; the ingredients are finely chopped and served chilled.

**Guiso de caracoles**: main course. Stewed snails with small pieces of Sierra ham, tomatoes, bell peppers, garlic, almonds, and pine nuts.

**Guiso de rabo de toro**: main course. A stew of bull's tail cooked with tomato, onion and pepper. The ingredients are soaked in *Montilla* which is a local wine.

**Huevos a la flamenca**: main course. Fried eggs served with a sauce of peas, ham, tomato, and beans.

**Olla gitana**: side dish. Plate of mixed vegetables, French beans, potatoes, bell peppers, tomatoes with chick-peas, pears, and almonds, seasoned with vinegar, oil and mild paprika.

**Pollo al Jerez**: main course. Chicken cooked in Jerez wine with mushrooms and onions.

**Riñones al Jerez**: main course. Kidney and onion cooked in the region's local Jerez wine.

## ASTURIAS AND CANTABRIA

We have decided to cover these two regions together since they encompass a single culinary zone, even though they are completely different from a historical, political, and social point of view.

Gastronomically speaking, Asturias is best known for its *fabada asturiana*; the zone is rich in fish, meat, and sliced ham and salami.

Cantabria enjoys an extremely varied, fish-based cuisine, although it is also rich in cheeses; butter is typically found in the rice-based dishes.

**Angulas a la cazuela**: main course. Eel fry cooked with garlic, oil, and chili pepper in small earthenware pans.

**Caldereta asturiana**: all-in-one dish: A mixture of small cuts of fish, mussels, clams, prawns, *centollo*, lobster, scampi, and limpets, cooked with wine, nutmeg, chili pepper, *pimentón*, onion, bell peppers, lemon, garlic, and parsley.

**Estofado a la asturiana**: main course. Beef stew cooked in lard with abundant vegetables and various herbs and spices.

**Estofado de buey** (Beef stew): main course. Dish prepared with leg of ox, but also with beef and vegetables. The dish is served with the meat in the center surrounded by the vegetables.

**Fabada asturiana**: starter. A somewhat heavy dish consisting of beans, *lacón*, lard, *morcilla*, onion, and salami.

**Fabes con almejes**: main course. Mixed dish of clam marinade, mussels, and beans, seasoned with parsley, bay leaf, onion, garlic, and saffron with a sprinkling of breadcrumbs.

**Frixuelos**: dessert. A kind of flapjack made with flour, egg, sugar, aniseed, salt, and oil.

**Merluza a la sidra** (Cidered hake): main course. Cooked in the oven, the hake is covered in a sauce of potatoes, tomatoes, and abundant cider.

**Morros de ternera a la asturiana**: main course. Spicy stew of snout and leg of veal, diced ham, onion, garlic, and walnuts.

**Pollo campurriano**: main course. Chicken chopped into pieces with rice and vegetables. A fairly heavy dish in that it contains abundant onion and lard.

## BALEARIC ISLANDS

The islands offer a rich variety of cuisine. Typical are the soups and pork, the latter being used in the excellent *sobrasada*.

**Burrida de ratjada**: main course. Skate stewed in an almond sauce.

**Caldereta de langosta**: all-in-one dish. Pieces of lobster with green bell peppers, eggs, and tomatoes.

**Caracoles pagesos**: main course. Snails cooked in wine and vinegar with herbs and spices.

**Carne de cerdo con leche**: main course. Pork cooked in milk with garlic and mild paprika and served with a potato or chestnut purée.

**Coca**: all-in-one dish. Thick pizza garnished in a host of different ways: typical topping consists of red bell peppers and black olives.

**Cuinat**: side dish. A purée of vegetables and pulses, broad beans, dried lupines, chard, the leaves of a wild plant known as *Lychnis*, and mint; usually eaten in springtime.

**Empanadas**: Folded-over pizzas containing fish, meat, or chard with pine nuts and raisins, sold in bakeries, pastry shops, and bars.

**Ensaimadas**: Round brioche made with a light pastry and filled with *cabellos de angel*, pumpkin jam.

**Flaó**: dessert. A tart garnished with a cream of fresh cheese, eggs, sugar, and mint.

**Lentejas con sobrasada**: starter. Lentils to which fried *sobrasada* is added.

**Sopa seca mallorquina**: starter. Similar to a pie, but cooked in a earthenware casserole dish. The ingredients are bread and vegetables.

**Tombet de peix**: main course. A kind of mixed timbale with fish and vegetables baked in the oven.

## CANARY ISLANDS

Geographically distant from the rest of Spain, it is not surprising to find that the cuisine is exotic with North African influences. For this reason it is difficult to find a common link between the culinary traditions of the peninsula and these wonderful islands.

**Escaldón canario**: main course. Fricassee of vegetables mixed with *gofio* (toasted wheat flour prepared with water or milk, salt or sugar).

# REGIONAL DISHES

**Puchero canario**: all-in-one dish. A mixed broth of meat and vegetables: the main ingredients are beef, chick-peas, potatoes, salami, zucchini, cabbage, beans, and corn.

**Sancocho canario**: main course. A stew of dried salted cod, potatoes, and sweet potatoes that is served with *salsa de mojo*, a sauce of breadcrumbs seasoned with garlic, oil, vinegar and cumin.

**Sopa del Teide**: starter. Simple risotto with ripe tomatoes, onion, and garlic.

**Tarta de plátanos**: dessert. Little balls of banana, egg, cinnamon, and sugar, fried and covered with honey.

## CASTILE-LEÓN

The gastronomic tradition of this region is firmly based on meat. Spring lamb and pig are the main ingredients of Castilian cuisine. However, fish are also an important element, obviously the freshwater kind and above all trout. Frogs and crabs are considered a great delicacy. Pork is the king of Castilian cuisine and there is no shortage of cold cuts and other pork cuts.

**Arroz a la zamorana**: starter. A fairly heavy dish, so much so that it is sometimes considered an all-in-one dish. It is a risotto cooked with parts of the pig such as the ear, snout, etc. to which are added onion, ham, and *navo* (a kind of celery).

**Caldereta de Cordero**: main course. A traditional dish cooked over a wood fire. The ingredients are pieces of spring lamb with brain, liver, and a host of spices.

**Cangrejos de río** (River crabs): starter. The crabs are cooked in a sauce of tomato, cognac, and abundant pepper and chili pepper.

**Cochinillo asado**: main course. Suckling pig roasted in lard.

**Judiones de la granja**: starter. Broad beans prepared with pig's trotter and ear plus small pieces of ham and salami.

**Lechazo castellano**: main course. Suckling lamb cooked in a earthenware saucepan with a little lard.

**Sopa castellana**: starter. A soup of bread with fried raw ham, beaten egg and abundant *pimentón*.

## CASTILE-LA MANCHA, MADRID, ESTREMADURA

The cuisine of these regions shares some common characteristics. We have therefore decided to group them together. Here you will find those farmhouse recipes of olden times that are followed to the letter. Without a doubt, these are what Spanish cuisine truly stands for.

**Besugo a la madrileña** (Sea bream a la madrilena): main course. Baked in the oven and served with a tomato purée.

**Cazuela extremeña**: main course. Pork stewed with *chorizo*, bell peppers, tomato and garlic.

**Caldereta extremeña**: main course. Kid or lamb and calf's liver simmered with onion, garlic, red win and flour, to thicken the sauce.

# REGIONAL DISHES

**Callos a la madrileña**: main course. Ox tripe, *chorizo*, *morcilla*, and ham cooked in oil, lard and white wine with onions, carrots, garlic, herbs, and spices.

**Cocido madrileño** (or **castellano**): main course. A dish of mixed boiled meats (chicken, breast, pig's trotters, ears, *morcilla*) with boiled vegetables served separately, carrots, potatoes, cabbage, onion, celery, and leeks, chick-peas in their own liquid. The broth is served in a tureen with *fideos* (fine noodles chopped into shorter lengths).

**Gratinado de berenjenas**: (Eggplant au gratin): side dish. Sliced eggplant covered in grated cheese and cooked in the oven.

**Las mijas**: dessert. Crustless bread fried in butter with raisins.

**Lentejas al estilo de Burgos**: main course. A stew of lentils and *morcilla* from the city of Burgos that is made from pig's blood, chopped onion and rice.

**Morteruolo**: a very particular dish. The ingredients are pieces of hare, chicken, pig's liver, lard, and cinnamon; they are all cooked together then finely chopped and covered in more lard.

**Perdiz estofada**: main course. Casseroled partridge with potatoes.

**Pisto manchego**: main course. Mixed fry of red bell peppers, potatoes, zucchini, tomatoes, and bacon.

**Rebado de Cáceres**: starter. Dried salted cod with potatoes and chopped hard-boiled egg yolks.

## CATALONIA

Catalonian cuisine differs from that of the other regions since it is particularly rich in products from both sea and mountain: from fish to meat including game; from vegetables to rich salads, not to mention the wide variety of sliced ham and cold cuts.

**Conejo con peras** (Rabbit and pears): main course. Small pieces of rabbit with a sauce of carrots, pears, leeks, and celery.

**Escalvida**: side dish. A selection of fried vegetables with bell peppers, eggplant, tomatoes, onions, potatoes, vinegar, and pepper.

**Escudella i carn d'olla**: all-in-one dish. This dish is made up of two parts. *Escudella* is a mixture of boiled meats (beef, pork, *butifarra*, etc.) with carrots, celery, chick-peas, potatoes, and cabbage; *pelota*, on the other hand, is a sort of meatball of lean minced meat with pepper, garlic, parsley, bread, flour, and salt, that is added to the *escudella* just before cooking is complete.

**Suquet de peix**: main course. A delicious selection of fish and shellfish served with a special almond sauce, fried bread, and liver of angler fish.

## GALICIA

From a gastronomic point of view, this region is often considered the home of seafood. Whilst this is certainly the case, other treats are also in store. Besides the specialties of fish, you will often find meat, and, in particular, game.

The salmon is quite excellent, as is the sea trout and red meat. In homes and restaurants there is no shortage of wonderful dishes of game such as duck or loin of wild boar.

Besides all this, pastries are absolutely delicious, in particular *las filloas*, that are a typical carnival dessert.

**Caldeirada (o caldareta) de pescado**: starter. A fish soup that consists of mackerel and angler fish cooked in white wine with garlic, tomato, and saffron; it is served with toasted bread.

**Caldo gallego** (Galician broth): starter. Two varieties of this broth exist; one vegetable, whilst the other is a lot richer and contains pig's tail and ear, *lacón* and the famous Galician variety of *chorizos*.

In the vegetable variety we find savoy, broad beans, beans, and potatoes. This special dish is somewhat heavy and whilst considered a starter, it could also be an all-in-one dish.

**Empanada gallega**: all-in-one dish. Savory pie filled with tuna or meat, vegetables, bell peppers, olives.

**Filloas**: dessert. Like *frixuelos* (see page 42), they are very thin *crêpes* filled with cream or pig's blood. It was originally is a dish traditionally eaten at carnival time.

**Lacón con grelos**: all-in-one dish. A heavy, spicy dish due to the presence of *lacón* with turnips, salami, pig's ear, and potatoes that are all boiled together. A traditional dish that is usually eaten in wintertime.

**Mejillones al vino blanco** (Mussels in white wine sauce): hors-d'oeuvre. Boiled mussels with a sauce of garlic, parsley, and white wine.

**Pulpo afeira**: main course. Octopus cooked in a previously prepared mixture of oil, garlic, hot and mild paprika, and left to brown.

**Rape a la gallega** (Galician style angler fish): main course. Angler fish cooked with potatoes, onion, and bay leaf.

**Reo con almejas** (Sea trout and clams): main course. The fish is cooked with wine and clams and is filleted and cut into slices before serving.

**Salmón a noso estilo** (Salmon): main course. Oven-baked salmon with mushrooms, meat stock, orange juice, and Tabasco sauce. It is served with a slice of raw ham on top.

**Vieiras con col**: main course. The shellfish are grilled, whilst the savoy cabbage is cooked with butter and white wine. Everything is then put in the oven before serving.

## BASQUE COUNTRY

Both national and international opinion have awarded Basque cuisine the number one spot on the Iberian peninsula.

A distinction can be made between the cuisine of the coastal areas, that is mainly fish-based (the most important ingredient being dried salted cod), and the inland cuisine that is heavily based on meat.

Besides these two important branches, there is also that

modern school known as *nouvelle cuisine*, a polished abstract of the region's gastronomic tradition, that has taken Basque chefs to the top of the culinary tree.

**Angulas a la vasca** (Basque-style eel fry): main course. The tiny eels are cooked one by one with garlic. Chili pepper is added afterwards. They are served together on a single plate.

**Bacalao al pil pil** (Dried salted cod) main course. This dish is served with a creamy sauce which is made by patiently stirring the ingredients in a saucepan. Essential for this delicious cream is the jelly obtained from the skin of the dried salted cod.

**Bacalao a la vizcaina**: main course. The dried salted cod is cooked in an earthenware pot with abundant onion and garlic. Hard-boiled egg yolks are also added.

**Cordero en chilindrón**: main course. Fricassee of lamb (or chicken) in a spicy sauce of onion, garlic, and thin strips of pepper.

**Chipirones en su tinta**: main course. *chipirón* is the name given to a small squid that is cooked in its own black ink sauce and served with rice.

**Chipirones rellenos**: main course. The same small squid filled with onion, bell peppers, tomato, breadcrumbs, and garlic, stewed in their own black ink sauce.

**Gallina en pepitoria**: main course. Fricassee of chicken in lard and oil with diced Sierra ham, white wine, and aromatic herbs. It is served with a sauce made from the juices accumulated during cooking mixed with egg yolk, garlic, and ground almonds.

**Merluza a la vasca**: main course. Slices of hake with prawns and clams in a thick white wine sauce, garlic, and parsley, garnished with boiled eggs, asparagus, and peas.

**Perdices con chocolate**: main course. Partridge in a sauce of cocoa, white wine, cloves, and other spices.

**Purrusalda**: main course. Dried salted cod with leeks and potatoes, and cooked in an earthenware casserole dish.

**Txangurro relleno**: (Stuffed *centollo*) starter. The meat of this sea crab is cooked with cognac, butter, tomato, salt, and pepper. The mixture is then put back into the shell and served.

## LA RIOJA, ARAGÓN, NAVARRA

These three regions each have a different cuisine, but share many common characteristics, since the basic ingredients of all three are mutton and poultry along with vegetable produce. The trout, a freshwater fish typical of these parts, is now established at a national level. The spring lamb also has an important role, without forgetting the famous Navarra asparagus..

**Caracoles a la riojana** (Snails): main course. A dish peculiar to this region. The snails are cooked in a sauce of tomato, bell peppers, and ham.

**Cochifrito**: main course. Pieces of spring lamb fried with abundant onion and garlic. Added spices are pepper and *pimentón*. The lamb is served without a sauce.

**Chuletas a la aragonesa**: main course. Pork chops floured and browned in lard with garlic, white wine, chopped hard-boiled eggs, and tomato purée.

**Hinojos con jamón**: (Fennel and ham): main course. Fried and scrambled eggs with fennel and ham.

**Judías con chorizo**: main course. Butter beans cooked in lard with potatoes, pieces of salami, onions, and garlic.

**Olla podrida**: starter. A hearty soup of mixed meats, pork, chicken, partridge, *chorizo*, lard, and bacon, with vegetables.

**Patatas a la riojana**: main course. Potatoes and *chorizo* browned in garlic, onion, and hot chili pepper.

**Pencas de acelga gratinada**: side dish. Chard stems are a traditional vegetable of central Spain; they are often cooked in the oven *au gratin* with béchamel and cheese.

**Pochas a la Navarra**: main course. *Pochas* is the local name for French beans cooked with tail of spring lamb in an earthenware casserole dish with a host of spices.

**Pollo al chilindrón**: main course. Small pieces of chicken with tomatoes, bell peppers, zucchini, eggplant, carrots, peas, and ham.

**Recao de Binéfar**: first course. A dish of butter beans, potatoes, rice, and a host of spices.

**Truchas a la Navarra** (Navarra-style trout): main course. Trout fried in lard together with a slice of raw ham. Served with a sprinkling of lemon.

## VALENCIA AND MURCIA

Rice is the common characteristic linking the culinary traditions of Valencia and Murcia. In these regions the best risotto is to be found, preparad in a thousand different ways. This is the home of *paella*, the national dish. Besides the rice, we find dishes of fish and shellfish, but no less important is the meat, particularly the spring lamb. Game is also an important ingredient in the cuisine of these Mediterranean regions.

**Arroz amb fesols y naps**: starter. Rice with butter beans and turnips.

**Arroz con costra**: all-in-one dish. A risotto with chickpeas, chicken, *butifarra*, and eggs.

**Buñuelos de manzanas**: dessert. Apple fritters with brandy.

**Dorada a la sal**: main course. Gilthead bream baked in the oven with a covering of salt.

**Fideua**: all-in-one dish. Risotto containing various types of fish with a sauce of almonds, bread, saffron and *pimentón*. Everything is then mixed with potatoes and onions.

**Guisado de trigo**: main course. A roast of chick- peas, potatoes, French beans, zucchini, tomatoes and a host of spices. This dish was traditionally eaten on Maundy Thursday (the Thursday before Easter).

**Paella a la valenciana**: all-in-one dish or main course. Huge dish of mussels, crabs or king prawns, cuttlefish, boiled chicken and its broth, diced ham, peas, French beans, tomatoes, garlic, saffron, herbs, and spices; the rice is added towards the end of cooking.

**Pestiños**: dessert. A kind of croissant that is fried and soaked with honey. Traditionally eaten at Easter.

**Salpicón de Murcia**: main course. Barbecued dried salted cod, which is then finely chopped, cooked with potatoes, and covered in a sauce of onion, parsley, garlic, oil, and vinegar.

# GASTRONOMIC TERMS

The definitions listed in this chapter are those generally used in restaurants throughout Spain to indicate the most common methods of cooking and preparation that characterize the country's best-known dishes.

**Al agridulce**: This can readily be translated as "sweet-and-sour" and is used to indicate that the sauce contains both vinegar and sugar.

**Ali-oli**: Typical of the Catalonia region, but may now be found throughout the peninsula. It is a kind of thin mayonnaise with abundant chopped garlic.

**A la campesina**: generic term for a farmhouse-style dish containing full-flavored ingredients.

**A la cazuela**: indicates that the dish is cooked over a low heat in a earthenware casserole dish.

**Al gratén**: the Spanish equivalent of the commonly used French term *au gratin*. The term is used to indicate the method of preparation of various dishes. The food is covered in béchamel or breadcrumbs and cooked in the oven until forming a light golden crust.

**A las hierbas**: expression used when the dish is prepared with an abundance of mixed herbs and spices.

**Al horno**: term used to describe any dish that is cooked in the oven.

**A la importancia**: term used exclusively for potatoes and which merely means "French fries."

# GASTRONOMIC TERMS

**A la jardinera**: this term means that vegetables are added to the main ingredient and is often used in the case of soups.

**Al Jerez**: used to describe a dish cooked in the famous wine from Andalusia.

**A la marinera**: used to describe a dish whose ingredients include fish or other seafood.

**Al natural**: For our translation we must once again use a borrowed French term: *au naturel*. This may be used to describe a food that is uncooked, or cooked in the most natural or simplest way without additional ingredients.

**A la parrilla**: this merely means that the food is grilled and it is used for meat, fish and seafood.

**Al plato**: besides indicating the presence of eggs, this term is used to show that the food will be served in the same casserole dish in which it was cooked.

**Al vapor**: this means that the food is steamed and is used for vegetables, and sometimes shellfish, such as mussels and clams.

**A la vinagreta**: a sauce of onion, oil, vinegar, parsley, and hard-boiled egg.

**Bocadillo**: any type of bread roll.

**De la casa**: specialties of the house exclusive to a particular restaurant. It is worth asking the waiter to explain what they are. When referring to wine, it indicates that it will be served in a carafe or has been produced by the restaurant itself.

**En almíbar**: term used to describe any kind of tinned fruit in syrup. Also used for *torrijas* (see page 22), although in this case the exact term is *in almíbar*.

**En escabeche**: pickled in vinegar.

**En rodajas**: indicates any type of food served in thin slices.

**En salsa tártara**: Used for fish dishes and merely means "served with a tartar sauce."

**En salsa verde**: sauce used for meat and fish-based recipes. A simple recipe of oil, salt, and parsley.

**En su tinta**: term used for cuttlefish and squid that are cooked in their own black ink sauce.

**Fiambre**: a selection of any type of sliced ham or cold cuts.

**Pinchos**: small rolls to be found in any bar or coffee shop.

**Plato combinado**: term used to describe a simple mixed platter that can contain eggs, potatoes, salad, slices of meat, etc. This type of dish is commonly served in bars and coffee shops.

**Relleno/a**: any type of dish with a stuffing or filling.

**Revuelto**: indicates the presence of scrambled eggs mixed with some other ingredient such as asparagus, prawns, etc.

**Vegetariano**: this definition can be applied to a whole host of different recipes, but in every case it refers to vegetable-based dishes that do not contain meat, fish or cold cuts.

**ALMEJAS A LA MARINERA**

## Ingredients:

| | | |
|---|---|---|
| clams | 2 lb 3 oz | (1 kg) |
| garlic | 2 cloves | |
| onion | 1 | |
| flour | 1 tablespoon | |
| white wine | 1 glass | |
| white pepper, parsley,<br>salt, olive oil | | |

## Method:

Leave the clams to soak in salted water for a couple of hours, thus ensuring that all sand is removed.

Heat a little olive oil in a earthenware casserole dish; add chopped garlic and onion.

Allow to brown over a moderate flame.

Add flour, white wine, and a little water. Increase the heat and allow to boil.

Add the clams and cover with a lid so that the steam opens the clams.

Stir, taste, and when cooked add salt, pepper, and parsley. Serve at once.

**Note:** All recipes serve four.

## CALDO GALLEGO

### Ingredients:

| | | |
|---|---|---|
| water | 6 pints | (3 liters) |
| ham bone | 1 | |
| veal bone | 1 | |
| haricot beans | 4 oz | (100 g) |
| sliced potatoes | 2 lb 3 oz | (1 kg) |
| fat | 1 oz | (25 g) |
| a little cabbage or savoy | | |
| (other vegetables as desired) | | |

### Method:

Place the bones and haricot beans in a large saucepan
with salted water. When the beans are half-cooked,
remove the bones, add the potatoes, and leave to cook.
In another saucepan, place the savoy and other chosen
vegetables and bring to the boil. Then place the
vegetables in the first saucepan and mix with the potatoes
and beans. Finally, add the fat and allow to cook well.

## CALLOS

**Ingredients:**

| | | |
|---|---|---|
| *tripe* | 2 lb 3 oz | *(1 kg)* |
| *onion* | *1/2* | |
| *flour* | 1 tablespoon | |
| *mild* pimentón | 1 tablespoon | |
| *hot* pimentón | 1 tablespoon | |
| *garlic, tomato, a little lard, salt* | | |

**Method:**

Cut the tripe into small pieces and leave to boil in a saucepan containing plenty of water. When the tripe is almost cooked, prepare a frying pan with a little lard, tomato, chopped garlic and onion, mild *pimentón*, hot *pimentón*, and the flour. Allow to fry until brown. Add the tripe and a little of its cooking water and leave until cooking is complete.

## COCIDO MADRILEÑO

### Ingredients:

| | | |
|---|---|---|
| chick peas | 1 lb | (1/2 kg) |
| cabbage or savoy | | |
| pork bone | 1 | |
| red salami sausage | 1 | |
| mixed meat | 11 oz | (300 g) |
| thin pasta, a little lard, salt | | |

### Method:

Place all the ingredients, except the pasta, in a pressure cooker and allow to boil for 30 minutes. Using the broth obtained, prepare a soup adding a thin type of pasta (either the long or short variety is OK). Serve the other ingredients on a separate platter with some olive oil.

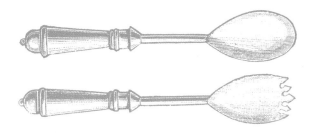

## Fabada Asturiana

### Ingredients:

| | | |
|---|---|---|
| *pig's trotter* | *1* | |
| *salted pork* | *1 lb* | *(1/2 kg)* |
| *pig's ear* | *1* | |
| *butter beans* | *2 lb 3 oz* | *(1 kg)* |
| *red salami sausages* | *3* | |
| *morcillas* | *3* | |
| *lard, salt, garlic, bay leaf* | | |

### Method:

Leave the trotter, meat, and ear to soak for 12 hours (change the water at least once). Transfer everything to a saucepan with the salami sausages, *morcillas*, and lard. Cover with a layer of butter beans and add chopped garlic, parsley, and quartered onion. Cover with cold water and bring to a boil, then reduce heat and cook slowly.

The beans should remain covered, so add more cold water if necessary. Cook until the beans are tender, and add a knob of butter before serving.

### MERLUZA A LA CAZUELA

### Ingredients:

| | | |
|---|---|---|
| *sliced hake* | *1 lb 6 oz* | *(600 g)* |
| *clams* | *11 oz* | *(300 g)* |
| *prawns* | *4 oz* | *(100 g)* |
| *white wine* | *1 glass* | |
| *flour* | *1 tablespoon* | |
| *onion, garlic,* pimentón, | | |
| *bay leaf, salt, olive oil* | | |

### Method:

Heat the oil in an earthenware casserole dish, add the garlic and onion, and allow to fry until brown; then add the clams and prawns and wait for the clams to open. Add the hake, *pimentón*, flour, bay leaf, and wine. Leave to cook over a moderate flame, and when cooking is complete, garnish with asparagus, bell peppers, and a sprig of parsley.

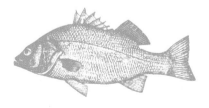

**PAELLA VALENCIANA**

## Ingredients:

| | | |
|---|---|---|
| rice | 7 oz | (200 g) |
| (1 coffee cup per person) | | |
| clams | 9 oz | (250 g) |
| prawns | 5 oz | (150 g) |
| cuttlefish cut into | | |
| small pieces | 5 oz | (150 g) |
| mussels | 5 oz | (150 g) |
| bell peppers | 2 oz | (50 g) |
| peas | 2 oz | (50 g) |
| finely chopped tomatoes | 2 | |
| sachets saffron | 3 | |
| finely chopped onion | 1 | |
| garlic cloves | 2 | |
| salt | | |
| stock cube | 1 | |

## Method:

Boil the mussels separately. When cooked, remove one half of each shell for decoration. In a large shallow pan (so much the better if you have the proper *paellera* that is specially designed for this dish) heat the oil and fry onion, garlic, parsley, and the tomatoes.

Once they are golden brown, add the prawns (leaving aside 4 of them for final decoration), the chopped cuttlefish, and the clams, and cook until the latter have opened.

Then add the bell peppers (that have been boiled beforehand), peas, and water: the secret of cooking the *paella* lies right here: three parts of water to one part of rice.

Add salt, the sachets of saffron, and the stock cube. When the water begins to boil, introduce the rice.

Important tip: the rice must on no account be stirred with a spoon. Instead, clasp the pan firmly by the handles, mixing the rice in a circular movement. Cooking time is about 30 minutes, but the *paella* will only be ready when all the water has evaporated.

Ten minutes before the end of cooking, arrange the remaining prawns and mussels as decoration. Slices of hard-boiled egg can also be added if desired. Serve at once.

Mixed paella also contains pieces of meat (chicken, beef, rabbit, etc. as desired) that are cooked separately and added just before the rice itself is fully cooked.

## Tortilla Española

### Ingredients:

| | | |
|---|---|---|
| *thinly sliced potatoes* | *3 lb 4 oz* | *(1 1/2 kg)* |
| *chopped onion* | *1* | |
| *eggs* | *4* | |
| *salt, olive oil* | | |

### Method:

Fry the potatoes and onion in a frying pan with a generous amount of olive oil. Beat the eggs in a bowl with a little salt. When the potatoes are cooked, transfer them to the bowl. Remove all the oil from the frying pan and introduce the mixture which should be cooked until golden brown on both sides. Serve at once.
If you want to try *tortilla paisana*, just fry a few zucchini and bell peppers along with the potatoes.

# ALPHABET

**A** como en **Antonio**
*ah kohmoh ayn ahntohnyoh*

**B Barcelona**
*bay bahrthehlohnah*

**C Carmen**
*thay kahrmayn*

**CH Chocolate**
*chay chohkohlahtay*

**D Dolores**
*day dohlohrays*

**E Enrique**
*ay aynreekay*

**F Francia**
*ehfay frahnthyah*

**G Gerona**
*khay khehrohnah*

**H Historia**
*achay eestohryah*

**I Inés**
*ee eenays*

**J José**
*khota khohsay*

**K Kilo**
*ka keeloh*

**L Lorenzo**
*ehlay lohraynthoh*

**LL Llobregat**
*aylyay lyohbraygaht*

**M Madrid**
*ehmay mahdreedh*

**N Navarra**
*ehnay nahvahrrah*

**Ñ Ñoño**
*aynyay niohnioh*

**O Oviedo**
*oh ohvyaydhoh*

**P París**
*pay pahrees*

**Q Querido**
*koo kayreedhoh*

**R Ramón**
*ehray rahmon*

**S Sábado**
*ehsay sahbhahdhoh*

**T Tortilla**
*tay torteelyah*

**U Ulises**
*oo ooleesays*

**V Valencia**
*oobay bahlaynthyah*

**W Washington**
*ooblay dohblay wahzeenton*

**X Xiquena**
*aykees kseekaynah*

**Y Yegua**
*ee greeayga yehkhwah*

**Z Zumo**
*thaytah thoomoh*

*Things to remember*

> If you want to purchase cheese or cold cuts, your best bet are the charcuterias. For other local products (wines, olive oil, etc.) the big supermarkets offer good quality and value for money.

Is this cheese fresh?

**¿Es fresco este queso?**
*Ays frayhskoh aystay kaysoh?*

How much does it cost per kilo?

**¿Cuánto cuesta al quilo?**
*Kwahntoh kwaystah ahl keeloh?*

How long will it keep?

**¿Cuánto tiempo dura conservado?**
*Kwahntoh tyaympoh doorah kohnsayrbahdoh?*

I'll take this/that

**Me llevo esto/eso**
*May lyayvoh aystoh/aysoh*

I'd like two bottles (of it)

**Querría/Quisiera dos botellas**
*Kayrryah /Keesyayrah dos bohtaylyahs*

Give me half a kilo (of it)

**Déme medio quilo**
*daymay maydhyoh keeloh*

Can you wrap it up for the journey?

**¿Me lo puede envolver para el viaje?**
*May loh pwaydhay aynbohlvayr pahrah ayl beeahkhay?*

# CAKESHOP

*Things to remember*

Cakeshops produce and sell a wide range of quality sweets and pastries which you will certainly want to try.

What are these/those? | **¿Qué son éstos / ésos?**
*Kay son aystohs / aysohs?*

What's in this cake? | **¿Qué tiene esta tarta?**
*Kay tyaynay aystah tahrtah?*

I'd like a small/medium tray of pastries | **Quisiera una bandeja pequeña / media de pasteles**
*Keesyayrah oonah bandaykhah paykayniah/ maydhyah day pahstaylays*

I'd like an assortment of pastries | **Quisiera pastas variadas**
*Keesyayrah pahstahs vahryahdhahs*

I'll have a 200-peseta cone, vanilla and chocolate with/without whipped cream | **Quisiera un cono de 200 pesetas con vainilla y chocolate con / sin nata**
*Keesyayrah oon kohnoh day dosthyayntahs paysaytahs kon bighneelyah ee chohkohlahtay kon / seen nahtah*

I'd like a 200-peseta ice-cream cup | **Quisiera una tarrina de helado de 200 pesetas**
*Keesyayrah oonah tahrreenah day aylahdhoh day dosthyayntahs paysaytahs*

68

| | |
|---|---|
| I have a small child/two children | **Tengo un niño pequeño/dos niños** *Tayngoh oon neenioh paykaynioh / dos neeniohs* |
| Do you have a special rate for children? | **¿Hacen precios reducidos para niños?** *Ahthen praythyohs raydootheedohs pahrah neeniohs?* |
| Do you have a cot/high chair for the baby? | **¿Tienen una cuna/una silla para el niño?** *Tyaynayn oonah koonah/oonah seelyah pahrah ayl neenioh?* |
| Is there a children's menu? | **¿Tienen un menú para niños?** *¿Tyaynayn oon maynoo pahrah neeniohs?* |
| Can you warm the baby's bottle? | **¿Puede calentarme el biberón para el niño?** *Pwaydhay kahlayntahrmay ayl beebhayron pahrah ayl neenioh?* |
| Where can I feed/change the baby? | **¿Dónde puedo dar la leche / cambiar al niño?** *¿Dohnday pwaydhoh dahr lah laychay/kahmbyahr ahl neenioh?* |
| Is there a park where the children can play? | **¿Hay un parque donde los niños puedan ir a jugar?** *Igh oon pahrkay dohnday los neeniohs pwaydhahn eer ah khoogahr?* |

# COMPLAINTS

| | |
|---|---|
| This doesn't work | **Esto no funciona**<br>_Aystoh noh foonthyonah_ |
| It's faulty | **Tiene algún defecto**<br>_Tyaynay ahlgoon dayfehktoh_ |
| We are still waiting to be served | **Estamos todavía esperando que nos sirvan**<br>_Aystahmohs tohdhahveeah ayspayrahndoh kay nohs seervahn_ |
| The coffee is cold | **El café está frío**<br>_Ayl kahfay aystah freeoh_ |
| The tablecloth is dirty | **El mantel no está limpio**<br>_Ayl mahntayl noh aystah leempyoh_ |
| The room is noisy | **En esta habitación se oyen todos los ruidos**<br>_Ayn aystah ahbheetahthyon say ohyayn tohdhohs los rooeedhos_ |
| It's too smoky here | **Aquí hay demasiado humo**<br>_Ahkee igh daymahsyahdhoh oomoh_ |

| | |
|---|---|
| Do you speak English? | **¿Habla inglés?**<br>*Ahblah eenglays?* |
| I don't speak Spanish | **No hablo español**<br>*Noh ahbloh ayspahniol* |
| What's your name? | **¿Cómo se llama / te llamas?**<br>*Kohmoh say lyahmah / tay lyahmahs?* |
| My name is... | **Me llamo...**<br>*May lyahmoh...* |
| Do you mind if I sit here? | **¿Le importa si me siento aquí?**<br>*Lay eempohrtah see may syayntoh ahkee?* |
| Is this place free? | **¿Está libre este sitio?**<br>*Aystah leebray aystay seetyoh?* |
| Where are you from? | **¿De dónde es?**<br>*Day dohnday ays?* |
| I'm from... | **Soy de...**<br>*Soy day...* |
| I'm English/American/<br>Spanish | **Soy inglés, americanos, español**<br>*Soy eenglays, ahmayreekahnohs, ayspahniol* |
| Can I offer you a coffee/<br>something to drink? | **¿Puedo invitarle a un café /algo de beber?**<br>*Pwaydhoh eenbeetahrlay ah oon kahfay/ahlgoh day baybhayr?* |

# CURRENCY

*Things to remember*

The peseta is the local currency with bank notes available
in the following denominations: 10,000 - 5,000 - 2,000 -
1,000. The range of coins is as follows: 500 - 200 - 100 -
50 - 25 - 5. You may occasionally find coins of a lesser
value but they are virtually worthless.

| | |
|---|---|
| I don't have enough money | **No tengo bastante dinero**<br>*Noh tayngoh bahstahntay deenayroh* |
| Do you have any change? | **¿Tienen para cambiar?**<br>*Tyaynayn pahrah kahmbyahr?* |
| Can you change a ten-thousand-peseta note? | **¿Me puede cambiar un billete de 10.000 pesetas?**<br>*May pwaydhay kahmbyahr oon beelyaytay day dyayth meel paysaytahs?* |
| I'd like to change these dollars/francs/sterling into pesetas | **Quisiera cambiar estos dólares/francos/estas esterlinas en pesetas**<br>*Keesyayrah kahmbyahr aystohs dohlahrays/frahnkos/aystahs aystayrleenahs ayn paysaytahs* |
| What is the rate for sterling/dollars/francs...? | **¿A cuánto está el cambio de las esterlinas/los dólares/los francos...?**<br>*Ah kwahntoh aystah ayl kahmbyoh day lahs aystayrleenahs/los dohlahrays/los frahnkos?* |

| First of March | **El 1 de marzo** | |
| | *Ayl oonoh day mahrthoh* | |

First of March — **El 1 de marzo** — *Ayl oonoh day mahrthoh*

Second of June — **Dos de junio** — *Dos day khoonyoh*

We will be arriving on the 29th of August — **Llegaremos el 29 de agosto** — *Lyaygahraymohs ayl 29 day ahgohstoh*

Nineteen ninety-seven — **Mil novecientos noventa y siete** — *Meel nohvaythyayntohs nohbayntah ee seeaytay*

| Sunday | **domingo** | *dohmeengoh* |
| Monday | **lunes** | *loonays* |
| Tuesday | **martes** | *mahrtays* |
| Wednesday | **miércoles** | *myayrkohlays* |
| Thursday | **jueves** | *khwayvays* |
| Friday | **viernes** | *byayrnays* |
| Saturday | **sábado** | *sahbhadhoh* |
| | | |
| January | **enero** | *aynayroh* |
| February | **febrero** | *fehbrehroh* |
| March | **marzo** | *mahrthoh* |
| April | **abril** | *ahbreel* |
| May | **mayo** | *mahyoh* |
| June | **junio** | *khoonyoh* |
| July | **julio** | *khoolyoh* |
| August | **agosto** | *ahgohstoh* |
| September | **septiembre** | *sehptyaymbray* |
| October | **octubre** | *oktoobray* |
| November | **noviembre** | *nohvyaymbray* |
| December | **diciembre** | *deethyaymbray* |

# DIRECTIONS

| | |
|---|---|
| Excuse me, where is the station? | **¿Perdone, dónde está la estación?** *Pehrdohnay dohnday aystah lah aystahthyon?* |
| How do I get to the airport? | **¿Cómo tengo que hacer para ir al aeropuerto?** *Kohmoh tayngoh kay ahthehr pahrah eer ahl ahayrohpwayrtoh?* |
| Is this the road that leads to Plaza Mayor? | **¿Es ésta la calle que va a la Plaza Mayor?** *Ays aystah lah kahlyay kay vah ah lah plahthah mahyohr?* |
| I'm looking for the tourist information office | **Estoy buscando la oficina de Información Turística** *Aystoy booskahndoh lah ohfeetheenah day eenformahthyon tooreesteekah* |
| How long does it take to get there? | **¿Cuánto se tarda en llegar?** *Kwahntoh say tahrdah ayn lyaygahr?* |
| Excuse me, can you tell me where the... restaurant is? | **¿Perdone, me puede decir dónde está el restaurante...?** *Pehrdohnay, may pwaydhay daytheer dohnday aystah ayl raystowrahntay...?* |

### Things to remember

*Besides coffee and other drinks, cafés also offer a selection of filled rolls, tapas, mixed platters, and pastries.*

| | |
|---|---|
| A black coffee/ cappuccino | **Un café solo / un café con leche** *Oon kahfay sohloh / oon kahfay kon laychay* |
| A draught beer | **Una cerveza de barril / una caña** *Oonah thehrbaythah day bahrreel/ oonah kahniah* |
| A medium lager/stout | **Una cerveza clara / oscura / media** *Oonah thehrbaythah klahrah ohskoorah/maydhyah* |
| Two cups of tea with milk | **Dos tazas de té con leche** *Dos tahthahs day tay kon laychay* |
| A glass of mineral water | **Un vaso de agua mineral** *Oon bahsoh day ahgwah meenayrahl* |
| With ice, please | **Con hielo, por favor** *Kon yayloh, por fahvor* |
| Another coffee, please | **Por favor, otro café** *Por fahvor, ohtroh kahfay* |
| Bring me the bill, please | **Tráigame la cuenta, por favor** *Trighgahmay lah kwayntah, por fahvor* |

*Things to remember*

Besides proper restaurants, there is also a range of other eating places including the *bodegas, tascas, tabernas, and mesones (small family-run restaurants).*

| | |
|---|---|
| Is there a good restaurant around here? | **¿Hay un buen restaurante por aquí?** *Igh oon bwayn raystowrahntay por ahkee?* |
| Is there a cheap restaurant nearby? | **¿Hay un restaurante barato por aquí cerca?** *Igh oon raystowrahntay bahrahtoh por ahkee thehrkah?* |
| Do you know of a restaurant with local cuisine? | **¿Puede indicarme dónde hay un restaurante que sirva comidas típicas?** *Pwaydhay eendeekahrmay dohnday igh oon raystowrahntay kay seervah kohmeedhahs teepeekahs?* |
| How does one get there? | **¿Cómo se llega?** *Kohmoh say lyaygah?* |
| Excuse me, can you tell me where is the ... restaurant? | **¿Perdone, me puede indicar dónde está el restaurante...?** *Pehrdohnay, may pwaydhay eendeekahr dohnday aystah ayl raystowrahntay...?* |

| | |
|---|---|
| Which is the best restaurant in town? | **¿Cuál es el mejor restaurante de la ciudad?** <br> *Kwahl ays ayl mehkhor raystowrahntay day lah thyoodhahdh?* |
| We'd like to eat in a cheap restaurant | **Queríamos comer en un restaurante que costase poco** <br> *Kayreeahmohs kohmehr ayn oon raystowrahntay kay costáse pohkoh* |
| Is it possible to book a table for four please? | **¿Se puede reservar una mesa para cuatro?** <br> *Say pwaydhay rehsayrbahr oonah maysah pahrah kwahtroh?* |
| I'd like to book a table for two people, for this evening/tomorrow evening at 8:00, in the name of... | **Quisiera reservar una mesa para dos personas, para esta noche/mañana por la noche a las ocho a nombre de...** <br> *Keesyayrah rehsayrbahr oonah maysah pahrah dos payrsohnahs, pahrah aystah nohchay/ mahniahnah por lah nohchay ah lahs ohchoh ah nohmbray day...* |
| What day are you closed? | **¿Cuándo es el día de descanso semanal?** <br> *Kwahndoh ays ayl deeah day descahnso semahnahl?* |

| | |
|---|---|
| What time does the restaurant open/close? | **¿A qué hora abre / cierra el restaurante?**<br>*Ah kay ohrah ahbray / thyehrrah ayl raystowrahntay?* |
| I'd like to cancel a booking I made for this evening, for two people, in the name of... | **Quisiera anular una reserva que había hecho para esta noche, para dos personas, a nombre de...**<br>*Keesyayrah ahnoolahr oonah rehsehrbah kay ahbeeah aychoh pahrah aystah nohchay, pahrah dos payrsohnahs, ah nohmbray day..* |
| Is it necessary to reserve? | **¿Es necesario reservar mesa?**<br>*Ays naythaysahryoh rehsayrbahr maysah?* |
| Good evening, a table for two | **Buenas noches, una mesa para dos**<br>*Bwaynohs nohchays, oonah maysah pahrah dos* |
| We'd like a table in a quiet corner | **Queríamos una mesa en un sitio tranquilo**<br>*Kayreeahmohs oonah maysah ayn oon seetyoh trahnkeeloh* |
| We've booked a table for two in the name of... | **Hemos reservado una mesa para dos, a nombre de...**<br>*Ehmohs rehsehrbahdhoh oonah maysah pahrah dos, ah nohmbray day...* |

Can one eat outside?

**¿Se puede comer fuera / al aire libre?**
*Say pwaydhay kohmehr fwayrah / ahl ighray leebray?*

We'd like a table away from/next to the window

**Queríamos una mesa lejos de / cerca de la ventana**
*Kayreeahmohs oonah maysah lehkhos day/thehrkah day lah behntahnah*

Is there an entrance for the disabled?

**¿Hay una entrada para minusválidos?**
*Igh oonah ayntradhah pahrah meenoosbahleedohs?*

Do you speak English, French...?

**¿Habla inglés, francés...?**
*Ahblah eenglays, frahnthays...?*

Is there a fixed-price menu?

**¿Tienen un menú con precio único?**
*Tyaynayn oon maynoo kon praythyoh ooneekoh?*

Can we see the menu?

**¿Podemos ver la carta?**
*Pohdehmohs behr lah kahrtah?*

Is there is vegetarian menu?

**¿Tienen un menú vegetariano?**
*Tyaynayn oon maynoo baykhaytahryahnoh?*

What is the specialty of the house?

**¿Cuál es la especialidad de la casa?**
*Kwahl ays lah ayspehthyahleedhahdh day la kahsah?*

# EATING OUT 5

| What is the dish of the day? | **¿Cuál es el plato del día?** <br> *Kwahl ays ayl plahtoh dayl deeah?* |
|---|---|
| What do you recommend? | **¿Qué nos recomienda?** <br> *Kay nohs rehkohmyayndah?* |
| What's in this dish? | **¿Qué lleva / tiene el plato?** <br> *Kay lyayvah / tyaynay ayl plahtoh?* |
| Is it spicy? | **¿Pica?** <br> *Peekah?* |
| I'm allergic to peppers | **Soy alérgico al pimiento** <br> *Soy ahlehrkheekoh ahl peemyayntoh* |
| Is there garlic/pepper in this dish? | **¿Este plato lleva ajo / pimienta?** <br> *Aystay plahtoh lyayvah ahkhoh / peemyayntah?* |
| Do you have...? | **¿Tienen...?** <br> *Tyaynayn...?* |
| I'd like/We'd like... | **Quisiera / Quisiéramos...** <br> *Keesyayrah / Keesyayrahmohs...* |
| Can you bring me/us...? | **Tráigame / nos...** <br> *Trighgahmay/ nohs...* |
| I would like a portion/half a portion of... | **Quisiera una ración / media ración de...** <br> *Keesyayrah oonah rahthyon/ maydhyah rahthyon day...* |

| | |
|---|---|
| I'd like to taste... | **Quisiera probar...** <br> *Keesyayrah provahr...* |
| Can you bring us some more bread please? | **¿Puede traernos más pan, por favor?** <br> *Pwaydhay trahehrnohs mahs pahn, por fahvor* |
| What are the typical local dishes? | **¿Cuáles son los platos típicos de la zona?** <br> *Kwahlays son los plahtohs teepeekohs day lah thohnah?* |
| What is the typical local cheese? | **¿Cuál es el queso típico de la zona?** <br> *Kwahl ays ayl kaysoh teepeekoh day lah thohnah?* |
| What dessert/fruit do you have? | **¿Qué postres / fruta tienen?** <br> *Kay pohstrays/ frootah tyaynayn?* |
| We'd like a portion of... and two plates | **Queríamos una ración de... con dos platos** <br> *Kayreeahmohs oonah rahthyon day... kon dos plahtohs* |
| Could I have the salt/ pepper? | **¿Me puede traer la sal / la pimienta?** <br> *May pwaydhay trahehr lah sahl / lah peemyayntah?* |
| Four coffees, please | **Cuatro cafés, por favor** <br> *Kwahtroh kahfays, por fahvor* |
| What starters are there? | **¿Qué entremeses tienen?** <br> *Kay ayntraymaysays tyaynayn?* |

I'd like this dish, but without onions

**Está bien este plato, pero sin cebollas**
*Ay<u>stah</u> byayn ay<u>stay</u> <u>plah</u>toh, <u>pay</u>roh seen thay<u>boh</u>lyahs*

Can you change the... for...?

**¿Puede cambiar el... por...?**
*Pway</u>dhay kahm<u>byahr</u> ayl... por...?*

Can we see the wine list?

**¿Podemos ver la carta de vinos?**
*Poh<u>deh</u>mohs behr lah <u>kahr</u>tah day <u>bee</u>nohs?*

We'd like an aperitif

**Queríamos un aperitivo/vermouth**
*Kay<u>ray</u>mohs oon ahpayree<u>tee</u>voh / behr<u>moot</u>*

What wine would you recommend with this dish?

**¿Qué vino nos recomienda para este plato?**
*Kay <u>bee</u>noh nohs rehkohm<u>yayn</u>dah pahrah ay<u>stay</u> <u>plah</u>toh?*

Can you recommend a good white/red/rosé wine?

**Recomiéndenos un buen vino blanco / tinto / rosado**
*rehkohm<u>yayn</u>daynohs oon <u>bwayn</u> <u>bee</u>noh <u>blahn</u>koh/ <u>teen</u>toh/ rosah<u>dhoh</u>*

We'd like the house wine, please

**Tráiganos el vino de la casa, por favor**
*<u>Trigh</u>gahnohs ayl <u>bee</u>noh day lah <u>kah</u>sah, por fah<u>vor</u>*

A/Half a bottle of...

**Una / Media botella de...**
*Oonah / maydhyah bohtaylyah day...*

A bottle of natural/
sparkling mineral
water, please

**Por favor, una botella de agua mineral natural / con gas**
*Por fahvor, oonah bohtaylyah day ahgwah meenayrahl nahtoorahl / kon gas*

We'd like some
unchilled/chilled water

**Queríamos agua del tiempo / del frigorífico**
*Kayreeahmohs ahgwah dayl tyaympoh/dayl freegohreefeekoh*

Another bottle of water/
wine please

**Por favor, tráiganos otra botella de agua /de vino**
*Por fahvor, trighgahnohs ohtrah bohtaylyah day ahgwah/ day beenoh*

Which are the typical
local wines/liqueurs?

**¿Cuáles son los vinos / los licores típicos de la zona?**
*kwahlays son los beenohs / los leekohrays teepeekohs day lah thohnah?*

What liqueurs do you
have?

**¿Qué licores tienen?**
*Kay leekohrays tyaynayn?*

Could we have the bill,
please?

**La cuenta, por favor**
*Lah kwayntah, por fahvor*

Excuse me, where is the restroom?

**¿Perdone, dónde está el baño?**
*Pehrdohnay, dohnday aystah ayl bahnioh?*

Can you bring me an ashtray / another glass / plate?

**¿Puede traerme un cenicero / otro vaso / plato?**
*Pwaydhay trahehrmay oon thayneethayroh /ohtroh bahsoh / plahtoh?*

Can you change my fork/knife/spoon please?

**¿Me cambia el tenedor/el cuchillo/la cuchara, por favor?**
*May kahmbyah ayl taynaydhohr/ayl koocheelyoh/lah koochahrah, por fahvor*

Can you turn the air conditioning up/down?

**¿Se puede bajar / subir el aire acondicionado?**
*Say pwaydhay bahkhahr / soobheer ayl ighray ahkohndeetheeohnahdoh?*

Is it possible to open/close the window?

**¿Se puede abrir / cerrar la ventana?**
*Say pwaydhay ahbreer/ thehrrahr lah behntahnah?*

I've stained my clothes, have you got any talcum powder?

**Me he manchado, ¿tienen polvos de talco?**
*May ay mahnchahdhoh, tyaynayn pohlbohs day tahlkoh?*

Could you call us a taxi please?

**¿Puede llamarnos a un taxi, por favor?**
*Pwaydhay lyahmahrnohs ah oon tahksee, por fahvor?*

| | |
|---|---|
| Is there a doctor here? | **¿Hay un médico aquí?**<br>*Igh oon mehdheekoh ahkee?* |
| Call a doctor/an ambulance | **Llamad / llamen a un médico / una ambulancia**<br>*Lyahmahdh/Lyahmayn ah oon mehdheekoh/oonah ahmboolahnthyah* |
| Go and get help, quickly! | **Id a pedir ayuda, ¡enseguida!**<br>*eed ah pehdheer ahyoodhah, aynsaygweedah!* |
| My wife is about to give birth! | **¡Mi mujer está pariendo!**<br>*Mee mookhehr aystah pahryayndoh!* |
| Where's the nearest police station/hospital? | **¿Dónde está la policía / el hospital más cercano?**<br>*Dohnday aystah lah pohleethyah/ ayl ohspeetahl mahs thehrkahnoh?* |
| I've lost my credit card/ wallet | **He perdido mi tarjeta de crédito / la cartera**<br>*Ay pehrdeedhoh mee tahrkhaytah day kraydheetoh/ lah kahrtayrah* |
| I've been robbed | **Me han robado**<br>*May ahn rohbhahdhoh* |
| My wallet has been stolen | **Me han robado la cartera**<br>*May ahn rohbhahdhoh lah kahrtayrah* |
| I've lost my child / handbag | **He perdido a mi hijo / el bolso**<br>*Ay pehrdeedhoh ah mee eekhoh / ayl bolsoh* |

| | |
|---|---|
| Are there any nightclubs/ pubs? | **¿Hay locales nocturnos/pubs?** *Igh lohkahlays nohktoornohs/pubs?* |
| Is there a show/place suitable for children? | **¿Hay algún espectáculo/ sitio adecuado para niños?** *Igh ahlgoon ayspehktahkooloh/ seeteeoh ahdhaykwahdoh pahrah neeniohs?* |
| What is there to do in the evenings? | **¿Qué se puede hacer por la noche?** *Kay say pwaydhay ahthehr por lah nohchay?* |
| Where is there a cinema/ theater? | **¿Dónde hay un cine/un teatro?** *Dohnday igh oon theenay/ oon tayahtroh?* |
| Can you book the tickets for us? | **¿Puede reservarnos las entradas?** *Pwaydhay rehsayrbahrnohs lahs ayntradhahs?* |
| Is there a swimming pool? | **¿Hay una piscina?** *Igh oonah peestheenah?* |
| Are there any good excursions to take? | **¿Hay buenas excursiones que hacer?** *Igh bwaynahs exkoorsyohnays kay ahthehr?* |
| Where can we play tennis/golf? | **¿Dónde podemos jugar a tenis/ a golf?** *Dohnday pohdehmohs khoogahr ah taynees / ah golf?* |
| Is there horseriding/ fishing? | **¿Se puede ir a caballo / a pescar?** *Say pwaydhay eer ah kahbhahlyoh / ah payskahr?* |

# GRAMMAR 1

## DEFINITE AND INDEFINITE ARTICLES

|  | Singular | Plural |
|---|---|---|
| the (M) | el | los |
| the (F) | la | las |
| a, some, any (M) | un | unos |
| a, some, any (F) | una | unas |

## NOUNS

As a rule, masculine singular nouns usually take the suffix **-o** (e.g. *chico*), whilst the feminine forms ends in **-a** (e.g. *chica*). However, certain masculine singular nouns end in **-e** (e.g. *padre*) or **-a** (e.g. *problema*).

There are also numerous nouns that finish in a consonant and may be either masculine (e.g. *camión, tenedor*) or feminine (e.g. *mujer, canción*).

The plural is formed as follows: nouns that end in a vowel take an **s** (e.g. *chico* becomes *chicos*), and those ending in a consonant take **es** (e.g. *camión* becomes *camiónes*).

## ADJECTIVES

The adjective must agree with the noun (e.g. *chico simpático - chicos simpáticos - chica simpática - chicas simpáticas*).

There are also several adjectives ending in **-e** that do not change with gender (e.g. *chico alegre, chica alegre*).

The plural forms follow the above-mentioned rule.

## POSSESSIVE ADJECTIVES

|  | *Singular* | *Plural* |
|---|---|---|
| my | mi | mis |
| your | tu | tus |
| his/her/its | su | sus |
| our | nuestro/nuestra | nuestros/nuestras |
| your | vuestro/vuestra | vuestros/vuestras |
| their | su | sus |

Examples: mi casa, su tinta, vuestros pollos

## POSSESSIVE PRONOUNS

|  | *Singular* | | *Plural* | |
|---|---|---|---|---|
|  | M | F | M | F |
| mine | el mío | la mía | los míos | las mías |
| yours | el tuyo | la tuya | los tuyos | las tuyas |
| his/hers/its | el suyo | la suya | los suyos | las suyas |
| ours | el nuestro | la nuestra | los nuestros | las nuestras |
| yours | el vuestro | la vuestra | los vuestros | las vuestras |
| theirs | el suyo | la suya | los suyos | las suyas |

## PRONOUNS

| *Subject* | *Direct Object* | *Indirect Object* | *Reflexive* |
|---|---|---|---|
| yo | me | me / A mí | me |
| tú | te | te / A ti | te |
| él | lo | le / A él | se |
| ella | la | le / A ella | se |
| usted | le | le / A Usted | se |

| nosotros/as | nos | nos / A nosotros/as | os |
| vosotros/as | os | os / A vosotros/as | os |
| ellos | los | les / A ellos | se |
| ellas | las | les / A ella | se |
| ustedes | les | les / A ustedes | se |

## VERBS

Spanish verbs can be divided into three conjugations as can be seen from the three verbs indicated below as examples.

### Simple present

| Amar | Comer | Escribir |
| (to love) | (to eat) | (to write) |
| am-o | com-o | escribo |
| am-as | com-es | escrib-es |
| am-a | com-e | escrib-e |
| am-amos | com-emos | escrib-imos |
| am-áis | com-éis | escrib-ís |
| am-an | com-en | escrib-en |

### Auxiliary verbs

| Ser | Haber |
| (to be) | (to have) |
| soy | he |
| eres | has |
| es | ha |
| somos | hemos |
| sóis | habéis |
| son | han |

## Other useful verbs

| Poder<br>(to be able) | Ir<br>(to go) | Ver<br>(to see) |
|---|---|---|
| pued-o | voy | veo |
| pued-es | vas | ves |
| pued-e | va | ve |
| pod-emos | vamos | vemos |
| pod-éis | vais | veis |
| pued-en | van | ven |

## Perfect tense

Unlike other languages such as French and Italian, Spanish has only one auxiliary verb HABER (to have). The past participle is invariable.

| he | amado | comido | escrito |
|---|---|---|---|
| has | amado | comido | escrito |
| ha | amado | comido | escrito |
| hemos | amado | comido | escrito |
| habéis | amado | comido | escrito |
| han | amado | comido | escrito |

| | |
|---|---|
| Hello | **Buenos días**<br>*Bwaynohs deeahs* |
| Good evening | **Buenas tardes/noches**<br>*Bwaynahs tahrdays/nohchays* |
| Good night | **Buenas noches**<br>*Bwaynahs nohchays* |
| Goodbye / See you soon | **Adiós / Hasta luego / Hasta pronto**<br>*Ahdeeohs / Ahstah lwaygoh / Ahstah prohntoh* |
| Pleased to meet you | **Mucho gusto**<br>*Moochoh goostoh* |
| How are you? | **¿Cómo está?**<br>*Kohmoh aystah?* |
| Fine, thank you | **Bien, gracias**<br>*Byayn, grahthyahs* |
| Please | **Por favor**<br>*Por fahvor* |
| Excuse me / I'm sorry | **Perdone / Lo siento**<br>*Pehrdohnay / Loh syayntoh* |
| Yes please/No thanks | **Sí, gracias / No, gracias**<br>*See, grahthyahs/ Noh, grahthyahs* |
| I would like/We would like... | **Quisiera/Quisiéramos...**<br>*Keesyayrah/Keesyayrahmohs...* |

*Things to remember*

> If you want to discover the real Spanish restaurants,
> remember to choose half board when making your hotel
> booking.

| | |
|---|---|
| I'd like to book a single/ double room | **Quisiera reservar una habitación individual / doble**<br>*Keesyayrah rehsayrbahr oonah ahbheetahthyon eendeeveedooahl /dohblay* |
| I'd like a room with breakfast/half board/ full board | **Quisiera una habitación con desayuno/media pensión /pensión completa**<br>*Keesyayrah oonah ahbheetahthyon kon daysahyoonoh/ maydhyah paynsyon / paynsyon kohmplaytah* |
| How much is it per night/week? | **¿Cuánto cuesta al día / a la semana?**<br>*Kwahntoh kwaystah ahl deeah / ah lah saymahnah?* |
| Does the price include breakfast? | **¿El desayuno está comprendido en el precio?**<br>*Ayl daysahyoonoh aystah kohmprayndeedhoh ayn ayl praythyoh?* |

We will be staying for three nights from... to...
**Nos quedamos por tres noches desde el... hasta el...**
*Nohs kaydahmohs por trays nohchays daysday ayl... ahstah ayl...*

We will arrive at...
**Llegaremos a las...**
*Lyaygahraymohs ah lahs...*

We've booked a room in the name of...
**Hemos reservado una habitación a nombre de...**
*Ehmohs rehsehrbahdhoh oonah ahbheetahthyon ah nohmbray day...*

Can you have my bags brought up to the room?
**¿Pueden llevarme el equipaje a la habitación?**
*Pwaydhayn lyayvahrmay ayl aykeepahkhay ah lah ahbheetahthyon?*

What time is breakfast/lunch/dinner?
**¿A qué hora es el desayuno / la comida / la cena?**
*¿Ah kay ohrah ays ayl daysahyoonoh/lah kohmeedhah/lah thaynah?*

Can we have breakfast in our room at... o'clock?
**¿Nos pueden traer el desayuno a las...?**
*¿Nohs pwaydhayn trahehr ayl daysahyoonoh ah lahs...?*

Can I have my key?

**Me puede dar mi llave?**
*¿May <u>pway</u>dhay dahr mee <u>lyah</u>vay?*

Please, put it on my bill

**Póngalo en mi cuenta**
*<u>Pohng</u>ahloh ayn mee <u>kwayn</u>tah*

I'd like an outside line, please

**¿Me puede dar la línea, por favor?**
*May <u>pway</u>dhay dahr lah <u>lee</u>nayah, por fah<u>vor</u>?*

Can I have another blanket/pillow?

**¿Me puede dar otra manta / otra almohada?**
*¿May <u>pway</u>dhay dahr <u>oh</u>trah <u>mahn</u>tah/<u>oh</u>trah ahlmoh<u>ah</u>dhah?*

I'm locked out of my room

**Me he quedado encerrado fuera de mi habitación**
*May ay kay<u>dah</u>dhoh aynthehr<u>rah</u>dhoh <u>fway</u>rah day mee ahbheetah<u>thyon</u>*

# NUMBERS 1

| | | | |
|---|---|---|---|
| 0 | **cero** *thayroh* | 14 | **catorce** *kahtorthay* |
| 1 | **uno** *oonoh* | 15 | **quince** *keenthay* |
| 2 | **dos** *dos* | 16 | **dieciséis** *dyaytheesays* |
| 3 | **tres** *trays* | 17 | **diecisiete** *dyaytheesyaytay* |
| 4 | **cuatro** *kwahtroh* | 18 | **dieciocho** *dyaytheeohchoh* |
| 5 | **cinco** *theenkoh* | 19 | **diecinueve** *dyaytheenwayvay* |
| 6 | **seis** *says* | 20 | **veinte** *bayntay* |
| 7 | **siete** *syaytay* | 21 | **veintiuno** *baynteeoonoh* |
| 8 | **ocho** *ohchoh* | 22 | **veintidós** *baynteedhos* |
| 9 | **nueve** *nwayvay* | 23 | **veintitrés** *baynteetrays* |
| 10 | **diez** *dyayth* | 30 | **treinta** *trayntah* |
| 11 | **once** *onthay* | 31 | **treinta y uno** *trayntah ee oonoh* |
| 12 | **doce** *dohthay* | 40 | **cuarenta** *kwahrayntah* |
| 13 | **trece** *traythay* | 50 | **cincuenta** *theenkwayntah* |

| | | | |
|---|---|---|---|
| 60 | **sesenta** *saysayntah* | 110 | **ciento diez** *thyayntoh dyayth* |
| 70 | **setenta** *saytayntah* | 200 | **doscientos/as** *dosthyayntohs/ahs* |
| 80 | **ochenta** *ohchayntah* | 300 | **trescientos/as** *traysthyayntohs/ahs* |
| 90 | **noventa** *nohvayntah* | 1000 | **mil** *meel* |
| 100 | **cien** *thyayn* | 2000 | **dos mil** *dos meel* |
| 101 | **ciento uno** *thyayntoh oonoh* | 1,000,000 | **un millón** *oon meelyon* |

| | | | |
|---|---|---|---|
| 1st | **primero** *preemehroh* | 6th | **sexto** *sehkstoh* |
| 2nd | **segundo** *saygoondoh* | 7th | **séptimo** *sehpteemoh* |
| 3rd | **tercero** *tehrthayroh* | 8th | **octavo** *ohktahvoh* |
| 4th | **cuarto** *kwahrtoh* | 9th | **noveno** *nohvehnoh* |
| 5th | **quinto** *keentoh* | 10th | **décimo** *daytheemoh* |

*Things to remember*

Major credit cards are accepted in virtually all shops, hotels, and restaurants in large cities and tourist resorts. They are also widely used at filling stations and tollways.

How much is it? **¿Cuánto cuesta?**
*Kwahntoh kwaystah?*

Can I have the bill please? **¿Puede traerme la cuenta, por favor?**
*Pwaydhay trahehrmay lah kwayntah, por fahvor?*

Can I pay by credit card? **¿Puedo pagar con tarjeta de crédito?**
*Pwaydhoh pahkhahr kon tahrkhaytah day kraydheetoh?*

Do you accept checks / traveler's checks? **¿Aceptan cheques / traveler's cheques?**
*Ahthehptahn cheks / travelers cheks?*

Can I have a receipt please? **¿Me da el recibo, por favor?**
*May dah ayl raytheebhoh, por fahvor?*

Is service/VAT included? **¿Se incluye el servicio / el IVA?**
*Say eenklooway ayl sehrbeethyoh / ayl eebah?*

What's the total?

**¿Cuánto es todo?**
*Kwahntoh ays tohdhoh?*

Do I have to pay in
advance?

**¿Tengo que pagar por adelantado?**
*Tayngoh kay pahgahr por
ahdaylahntahdhoh?*

Do I have to leave a
deposit?

**¿Tengo que dejar un adelanto?**
*Tayngoh kay dehkhahr oon
ahdaylahntoh?*

I think you have given
me the wrong change

**Me parece que me ha dado la
vuelta equivocada**
*May pahraythay kay may ah
dahdhoh lah bwehltah
aykeevohkahdhah*

| | |
|---|---|
| Can you help me, please? | **¿Puede ayudarme, por favor?**<br>*Pwaydhay ahyoodharmay, por fahvor?* |
| What's the matter? | **¿Qué pasa?**<br>*Kay pahsah?* |
| I need help | **Necesito ayuda**<br>*naythayseetoh ahyoodhah* |
| I don't understand | **No entiendo**<br>*Noh ayntyayndoh* |
| Say it again, please | **¿Puede repetir, por favor?**<br>*Pwaydhay raypayteer, por fahvor* |
| I've got no money left | **Me he quedado sin dinero**<br>*May ay kaydahdhoh seen deenayroh* |
| I can't find my son/<br>daughter | **No encuentro a mi hijo / mi hija**<br>*Noh aynkwayntroh ah mee eekhoh / eekhah* |
| I'm lost | **Me he perdido**<br>*May ay pehrdeedhoh* |
| Leave me alone | **Déjame en paz**<br>*Daykhahmay ayn path* |

# PRONUNCIATION 1

It should firstly be pointed out that the Spanish alphabet has a few extra diacritical letters which contain signs used to indicate different sounds or values of the letter, e.g. **ñ**.

Below is a list giving pronunciation, approximate phonetic symbol and example for each letter. Unless otherwise stated, the pronunciation reads just as if it were English. Whilst the various sounds of the two languages do not correspond exactly, in following these guidelines you should have no difficulty in making yourself understood. Please note that you will occasionally find slight differences to this pattern, particularly in the case of foreign words or diphthongs.

The underlined syllable indicates the stress (or emphasis) on each particular word.

| Letter | Pronunciation | Phonetic symbol | Example | |
|--------|---------------|-----------------|---------|---|
| **Vowels** | | | | |
| a | like **ar** in p**ar**t, but quite short | ah | **carne** | _kahrnay_ |
| e | 1] may be like **a** in late | ay | **repollo** | _raypohlyoh_ |
|   | 2] occasionally like **e** in get | eh | **pierna** | _pyehrnah_ |
| i | 1] like **ee** in meet | ee | **limón** | _leemon_ |
|   | 2] in diphthongs like **y** in yes | y | **quisiera** | _keesyayrah_ |

| | | | | |
|---|---|---|---|---|
| **o** | 1] may be similar to **o** in v**o**te | oh | **horno** | _ohrnoh_ |
| | 2] can be like **o** in g**o**t | o | **melón** | may_lon_ |
| **u** | 1] like **oo** in b**oo**t | oo | **uvas** | _oo_vahs |
| | 2] in diphthongs like **w** in **w**ere | w | **cuanto** | _kwahntoh_ |
| **y** | only a vowel at the end of some words or alone; like **ee** in m**ee**t | ee y | **muy** | mwee |

**N.B.** **ay** like **igh** in h**igh**    igh    **hay**    _igh_

## Consonants

| | | | | |
|---|---|---|---|---|
| **f, k, l,**<br>**m, n, p,**<br>**t, x, y** | the same as English | | | |
| **b** | 1] usually as in English | b | **besugo** | bay_soo_khoh |
| | 2] in between vowels, a sound somewhere between **b** and **v** | bh | **caballa** | kahb_hah_lyah |
| **c** | 1] before **e** and **i** like **th** in **th**ick | th | **cebolla** | thay_boh_lyah |
| | 2] in other cases like **k** in **k**ing | k | **coco** | _koh_koh |
| **ch** | the same as English | ch | **lechuga** | lay_choo_khah |
| **d** | 1] usually as in **d**ark, however less decisive | d | **dulce** | _dool_thay |

|   | | | |
|---|---|---|---|
| | 2] between vowels and at the end of a word, like **th** in **th**is | dh **hígado** | _eechahdhoh_ |
| **g** | 1] before **e** and **i** like **ch** in lo**ch** | kh **gente** | _khayntay_ |
| | 2] In other cases, generally like **g** in **g**o | g **langosta** | _lahngohstah_ |
| **h** | always silent | **huevos** | _wayvohs_ |
| **j** | like **ch** in lo**ch** | kh **jámon** | _khahmon_ |
| **ll** | like **lli** in mi**lli**on | ly **ajillo** | _ahkheelyoh_ |
| **ñ** | like **ni** in o**ni**on | ni **coñac** | _cohniahk_ |
| **qu** | like **k** in **k**it | k **queso** | _kaysoh_ |
| **r** | a more emphatic trill, particularly with **rr** or at the start of a word | r **rosa** | _rosah_ |
| **s** | like the **s** in **s**it, but often with a slight lisp | s **pastas** | _pahstahs_ |
| **v** | 1] usually like **b** in **b**ig, but not so tense | b **venado** | _baynahdhoh_ |
| | 2] in between vowels it resembles an English **v** | v **favor** | _fahvor_ |
| **z** | like **th** in **th**ick | th **maíz** | _maheeth_ |

| New Year's Eve | **Nochevieja** <br> *Nohchaybyaykhah* |
|---|---|
| Good Friday | **Viernes Santo** <br> *Byayrnays Sahntoh* |
| Easter | **Semana Santa** <br> *Saymahnah Sahntah* |
| Christmas Eve | **Noche buena** <br> *Nohchay bwaynah* |
| Christmas | **Navidad** <br> *Nahbeedhadh* |
| Maundy Thursday | **Jueves Santo** <br> *Khwayvays Sahntoh* |
| Feast of the Immaculate Conception | **Inmaculada** <br> *Eenmahkoolahdhah* |

| | |
|---|---|
| Is it far? | **¿Está lejos?**<br>*Aystah lehkhos?* |
| Is it expensive? | **¿Cuesta mucho?**<br>*kwaystah moochoh?* |
| Can you help me? | **¿Puede ayudarme?**<br>*Pwaydhay ahyoodharmay?* |
| Have you understood? | **¿Ha entendido?**<br>*Ah ayntayndeedhoh?* |
| Where are the shops? | **¿Dónde están las tiendas?**<br>*Dohnday aystahn lahs tyayndahs?* |
| How do I get there? | **¿Cómo se llega allí?**<br>*Kohmoh say lyaygah ahlyee?* |
| What is this? | **¿Qué es esto?**<br>*Kay ays aystoh?* |

Where is the restroom please?

**¿Dónde está el baño, por favor?**
*Dohnday aystah ayl bahnioh, por fahvor?*

Do you have to pay for the toilets?

**¿El servicio del baño se paga?**
*Ayl sehrbeethyoh dayl bahnioh say pahgah?*

There's no toilet paper/soap

**No hay papel higiénico / jabón**
*Noh igh pahpehl eekhyayneekoh / khahbhon*

Is there a toilet for the disabled?

**¿Hay un baño para minusválidos?**
*Igh oon bahnioh pahrah meenoosbahleedhohs?*

The toilet is blocked

**El baño está obstruido**
*Ayl bahnioh aystah ohbstrooeedhoh*

# SMOKING

*Things to remember*

> Smoking in public places (museums, cinemas, etc.) and on public transport (buses, subways, etc.) is forbidden throughout Spain. Trains have special smoking compartments. In most restaurants there are no restrictions.

| | |
|---|---|
| Is smoking allowed here? | **¿Se puede fumar aquí?**<br>*Say <u>pway</u>dhay foo<u>mahr</u> ah<u>kee</u>?* |
| Do you mind if I smoke? | **¿Le molesta si fumo?**<br>*Lay moh<u>lay</u>stah see <u>foo</u>moh?* |
| Could I have an ashtray? | **¿Dónde hay un cenicero?**<br>*<u>Dohn</u>day igh oon thaynee<u>thay</u>roh?* |
| Do you have matches? | **¿Tienen / tenéis cerillas?**<br>*<u>Tyay</u>nayn/ tay<u>nays</u> the<u>ree</u>lyahs?* |
| Have you got a light? | **¿Tiene fuego?**<br>*<u>Tyay</u>nay <u>fway</u>goh?* |
| Would you mind not smoking? | **¿Le importaría dejar de fumar?**<br>*Lay eempohrtah<u>ree</u>ah deh<u>khahr</u> day foo<u>mahr</u>?* |

*Things to remember*

*All cities have authorized taxi firms that generally have white vehicles with a red stripe, although in Barcelona they are yellow and black. You are advised to avoid "private" taxis, but if left with no choice, make sure you agree on a price before setting off.*

| | |
|---|---|
| Can you call me a taxi please? | **¿Puede llamarme a un taxi, por favor?** <br> *Pwaydhay lyahmahrmay ah oon tahksee, por fahvor?* |
| To the main station/the airport | **A la estación central/al aeropuerto** <br> *Ah lah aystahthyon thayntrahl/ahl ahayrohpwayrtoh* |
| Take me to this address/ this hotel | **Lléveme a esta dirección/a este hotel** <br> *Lyayvaymay ah aystah deerehkthyon/ ah aystay ohtayl* |
| Is it far? | **¿Está lejos?** <br> *Aystah lehkhos?* |
| I'm in a hurry | **Tengo mucha prisa** <br> *Tayngoh moochah preesah* |
| How much will it cost? | **¿Cuánto me costará?** <br> *Kwahntoh may kohstahrah?* |
| Stop here/on the corner | **Párese aquí / en la esquina** <br> *Pahraysay ahkee/ayn lah ayskeenah* |
| How much is it? | **¿Cuánto es?** <br> *Kwahntoh ays?* |

# TELEPHONE 1

*Things to remember*

> Most public telephones take 100, 50, or 25-peseta coins, although cardphones are now commonplace. Phonecards can be purchased from tobacconists, newsstands, and special vending machines.

Is there a phone?
**¿Hay un teléfono?**
*Igh oon taylayfohnoh?*

I'd like an outside line
**¿Me pone línea?**
*May pohnay leenayah?*

Can I have a 500/1000-peseta phonecard?
**Déme una tarjeta telefónica de 500/1000 pesetas**
*Daymay oonah tahrkhaytah taylayfohneekah day keenyayntohs/meel paysaytahs*

I'd like to make a phone call
**Quisiera llamar por teléfono**
*Keesyayrah lyahmahr por taylayfohnoh*

The number is... extension...
**El número es... interno...**
*Ayl noomayroh ays... eentayrnoh...*

How much is it to phone the United States, England...?
**¿Cuánto cuesta llamar a Estados Unidos, Inglaterra...?**
*Kwahntoh kwaystah lyahmahr ah Aystahdhohs Ooneedhohs, Eenglahtehrrah...*

| | |
|---|---|
| I can't get through | **No consigo que me den linea**<br>*Noh konh<u>see</u>goh kay may dayn <u>lee</u>nayah* |
| What's the code for... | **¿Cuál es el prefijo de...**<br>*Kwahl ays ayl pray<u>fee</u>khoh day...* |
| Hello, this is... | **Soy...**<br>*Soy...* |
| Can I speak to...? | **¿Puedo hablar con...?**<br>*<u>Pway</u>dhoh ah<u>blahr</u> kon...?* |
| Could you give me some change in 25/50/100-peseta coins? | **¿Puede cambiármelos en monedas de 25 / 50 / 100 pesetas?**<br>*<u>Pway</u>dhay kahm<u>byahr</u>maylohs ayn moh<u>nay</u>dahs day baynteet<u>heen</u>koh/ theenk<u>wayn</u>tah/ thyayn pay<u>say</u>tahs* |
| It's busy | **Comunica**<br>*Kohmoo<u>nee</u>kah* |
| I've been cut off | **Me han cortado la llamada / la comunicación**<br>*May ahn kohr<u>tah</u>dhoh lah lyah<u>mah</u>dhah/lah kohmooneekah<u>thyon</u>* |
| It's a bad line | **No se oye bien**<br>*Noh say <u>oy</u>ay byayn* |
| I'm sorry, wrong number | **Perdone, me he equivocado de número**<br>*Pehr<u>doh</u>nay, may ay aykeevoh<u>kah</u>dhoh day <u>noo</u>mayroh* |

**YOU MAY HEAR:** ─────────────────────────

| | |
|---|---|
| Hello, who's speaking? | **¿Diga, quién es?**<br>_Deegah, kyayn ays?_ |
| Hold the line | **Permanezca en línea**<br>_Permanéthca ayn leenayah_ |
| Please try again later | **Inténtelo más tarde, por favor**<br>_Eentayntayloh mahs tahrday, por fahvor_ |
| He/she is not here | **No está**<br>_Noh aystah_ |
| You've got the wrong number | **Se ha equivocado de número**<br>_Say ah aykeevohkahdhoh day noomayroh_ |

| What time is it? | **¿Qué hora es?** | *Kay ohrah ays?* |
| It's... | **Son las...** | *Son lahs...* |
| x : 05 | **... y cinco** | *... ee theenkoh* |
| x : 10 | **... y diez** | *... ee dyayth* |
| x : 15 | **... y cuarto** | *... ee kwahrtoh* |
| x : 20 | **... y veinte** | *... ee bayntay* |
| x : 30 | **... y media** | *... ee maydhyah* |
| x : 40 | **... menos veinte** | *... maynohs bayntay* |
| x : 45 | **... menos cuarto** | *... maynohs kwahrtoh* |

| Eight A.M./P.M. | **Las ocho de la mañana/de la tarde**<br>*Lahs ohchoh day lah mahniahnah/day lah tahrday* |
| Midday | **Mediodía**<br>*maydhyohdheeah* |
| Midnight | **Las doce de la noche**<br>*Lahs dohthay day lah nohchay* |

| | |
|---|---|
| What time do you (does it) open/close? | **¿A qué hora abre / cierra ?** <br> *Ah kay ohrah ahbray /thyehrrah?* |
| What time does the restaurant close? | **¿A qué hora cierra el restaurante?** <br> *Ah kay ohrah thyehrrah ayl raystowrahntay?* |
| What time do the shops close? | **¿A qué hora cierran las tiendas?** <br> *Ah kay ohrah thyayrrahn lahs tyayndahs?* |
| How long will it take to get there? | **¿Cuánto se tardará en llegar?** <br> *Kwahntoh say tahrdahrah ayn lyaykhahr ?* |
| We arrived early/late | **Hemos llegado pronto / tarde** <br> *Ehmohs lyaykhahdhoh prohntoh / tahrday* |
| It's early/late | **Es pronto / tarde** <br> *Ays prohntoh/ tahrday* |
| The table is booked for... this evening | **La mesa está reservada para las... de esta noche** <br> *Lah maysah aystah rehsayrbahdah pahrah lahs... day aystah nohchay* |

*Things to remember*

As one might expect, it is common practice to tip in
hotels, the restaurant waiter, taxi driver, junior hairdresser,
etc. The customary amount is between 5 and 10% which
in most cases should work out a few hundred pesetas.

| | |
|---|---|
| I'm sorry, I don't have change | **Lo siento, no tengo suelto** *Loh syayntoh, noh tayngoh swayltoh* |
| Keep the change | **Tenga, la vuelta** *Tayngah, lah bwehltah* |
| Can you give me... in change | **¿Me puede dar... en monedas?** *May pwaydhay dahr... ayn mohnaydahs?* |
| Is the tip included? | **¿Está incluida la propina?** *Aystah eenklooeedhah lah prohpeenah?* |
| Take ... pesetas | **Cobre... pesetas** *Kohbray... paysaytahs* |

| | |
|---|---|
| Half a liter of... | **Medio litro de...**<br>*Maydhyoh leetroh day...* |
| A liter of... | **Un litro de...**<br>*Oon leetroh day...* |
| A kilo of... | **Un kilo de...**<br>*Oon keeloh day...* |
| Half a kilo of... | **Medio kilo de...**<br>*Maydhyoh keeloh day...* |
| 100 grams of... | **100 gramos de...**<br>*thyayn grahmohs day...* |
| A slice of... | **Un trozo de...**<br>*Oon trohthoh day...* |
| A portion of... | **Una porción / ración de...**<br>*Oonah porthyon/rahthyon day...* |
| A dozen... | **Una docena de...**<br>*Oonah dothehnah day...* |
| Two hundred pesetas' worth of... | **Doscientas pesetas de...**<br>*Dosthyayntahs paysaytahs day...* |

# GASTRONOMIC DICTIONARY

**a lot** mucho *moochoh*
**able, to be** poder *pohdhayr*
**above** encima *aynthymah*
**account** cuenta *kwayntah*
**ache** mal/dolor *mahl/dohlor*
**acid** ácido *ahtheedhoh*
**additive** aditivo *ahdeeteevoh*
**address** dirección *deeraykthyon*
**adult** adulto *ahdhooltoh*
**after** después *dayspways*
**against** contra *kohntrah*
**air** aire *ighray*
**air-conditioning** aire acondicionado *ighray ahkondeethyohnahdhoh*
**airplane** avión *ahvyon*
**airport** aeropuerto *ahayrohpwayrtoh*
**alcoholic** alcohólico *ahlkohohleekoh*
**alcoholic drinks** alcohólicos *ahlkohohleekohs*
**alert** atento *ahtayntoh*
**all** todo *tohdhoh*
**allergy** alergia *ahlehrkhyah*
**almonds** almendras *ahlmayndrahs*
**almost** casi *kahsee*
**also** también *tahmbyayn*

**always** siempre *seeaympray*
**amongst** entre *ayntray*
**anchovy** anchoa *ahnchohah*
**angle** ángulo *ahngooloh*
**announcement** comunicación *kohmooneekahthyon*
**antibiotic** antibiótico *ahnteebyohteekoh*
**any** cualquier/a *kwahlkyehr/ah*
**anything** algo *ahlgoh*
**aperitif** aperitivo *ahpayreeteevoh*
**appetite** apetito *ahpayteetoh*
**appetizer** entremés *ayntraymays*
**apple** manzana *mahnthahnah*
**appointment** cita *theetah*
**appreciate** aceptar con agrado *athayptahr kon agrahdhoh*
**apricot** albaricoque *ahlbahreekohkay*
**April** abril *ahbreel*
**aroma** aroma *ahrohmah*
**aromatic** aromático *ahrohmahteekoh*

**aromatic herbs** especias
*ayspaythyahs*

**around** alrededor
*ahlraydhaydhohr*

**arrive, to** llegar *lyaygahr*

**artichoke** alcachofa
*ahlkahchohfah*

**as** como *kohmoh*

**as far as** hasta *ahstah*

**ash** ceniza *thayneethah*

**ashtray** cenicero
*thayneethayroh*

**ask, to** pedir/ preguntar
*pehdheer* / *praygoontahr*

**asparagus** espárragos
*ayspahpahrrahgohs*

**aspirin** aspirina
*ahspeereenah*

**at least** al menos *ahl
maynohs*

**at once** enseguida
*aynsaygweedah*

**attentive** atento *ahtayntoh*

**August** agosto *ahgohstoh*

**authentic** auténtico
*owtaynteekoh*

**avocado** aguacate
*ahgwahkahtay*

**avoid, to** evitar *aybeetahr*

**baby carriage** carroza de
niños *carrothah day
neeniohs*

**baby food** homogeneizado
*ohmohkhaynaythadhoh*

**backwards** detrás *daytrahs*

**bacon, smoky** bacon
ahumado *baykon
ahoomahdhoh*

**bad** feo *fehoh*; **bad** mal/o
*mahl/mahloh*

**bag** bolso *bolsoh*

**baking** cocíón *cothyon*

**banana** plátano *plahtahnoh*

**Band Aid** tirita *teereetah*

**bank** banco *bahnkoh*

**bar** bar *bar*; **bar** local
*lohkahl*

**barbecue, to** cocer a la
brasa *kothayr ah lah
brahsah*

**barley** cebada
*thaybahdhah*

**barman** camarero del bar
*kahmahrayroh dayl bahr*

**basil** albahaca
*ahlbhahahkah*

**bass (fish)** lubina
*loobheenah*

**beans** alubias
*ahloobheeahs*

**beat, to** batir *bahteer*

**because** porque *porkay*

**beef** novillo *nohbeelyoh*;
bovino *bohbheenoh*

**beer** cerveza _thehrbaythah_;
 **bitter** c. oscura _th.
 skoorah_; **lager,** c. clara _th.
 klahrah_; **large beer,** c.
 grande _th. grahnday_; **small
 beer** c. pequeña _th.
 paykayniah_; **draught beer**
 caña _kahniah_

**beet, beetroot** remolacha
 _raymohlahchah_

**before** antes _ahntays_

**begin, to** comenzar
 _kohmaynthahr_

**behind** detrás _daytrahs_

**bell pepper** pimiento
 _peemyayntoh_

**beside** junto a.. _goontoh ah_

**best** mejor _mehkhor_

**better** mejor _mehkhor_

**between** entre _ayntray_

**big** grande _grahnday_

**bill** cuenta _kwayntah_

**biscuits** biscotes/ galletas
 _beeskohtays/gahlyaytahs_

**bitter** amargo _ahmahrgoh_;
 **bitter** áspero _ahspayroh_

**bitter liqueur** licor _leekor_

**black** negro _nehgroh_

**blend** mezcla _maythklah_

**boil, to** hervir _ehrbheer_

**boiled** cocido _kotheedhoh_

**bone** hueso _waysoh_

**book** libro _leebroh_

**book, to** reservar
 _rehsayrbahr_

**booked** reservado
 _rehsehrbahdhoh_

**booking** reserva _rehsayrbah_

**bottle opener** abrebotellas
 _ahbraybohtaylyahs_

**bottle** botella _bohtaylyah_

**bottled** embotellado
 _aymbohtaylyahdhoh_

**box** caja _kahkhah_

**boy** chico _cheekoh_

**brain** cerebro _thayraybroh_

**brandy** aguardiente
 _ahgwahrdyayntay_

**bread** pan _pahn_

**breadsticks** palitos de pan
 _pahleetohs day pahn_

**breadcrumbs** pan rallado
 _pahn rahlyahdhoh_

**breaded** empanado
 _aympaynahdhoh_

**break, to** romper _rohmpayr_

**breakdown** estropeado/
 destrozo _aystrohpayahdhoh/
 daystrohthoh_

**breakfast** desayuno
 _daysahyoonoh_

**bream, gilthead** dorada
 _dohrahdoh_

**breast** pecho _paychoh_

**bring, to** traer/llevar
_trah<u>eh</u>r/lyay<u>var</u>_

**broad beans** habas
_<u>ahb</u>bahs_

**broccoli** bréjoles
_<u>bray</u>khohlays_

**broken**
estropeado/destrozo/roto
_aystrohpay<u>ah</u>dhoh/
day<u>strohthoh/rohtoh</u>_

**broth** caldo _<u>kahl</u>dhoh_

**browned** dorado
_doh<u>rah</u>dhoh_; sofrito
_soh<u>free</u>toh_

**brush** cepillo _thay<u>pee</u>lyoh_

**Brussels sprout** repollo de
Bruselas _ray<u>pohl</u>yoh day
broo<u>say</u>lahs_

**burn, to** quemar _kay<u>mahr</u>_

**burnt** quemado
_kay<u>mah</u>dhoh_

**bus** autobús _owtoh<u>bhoos</u>_

**busy** ocupado
_ohkoo<u>pah</u>dhoh_

**butcher's** carnicería
_kahrneethay<u>ree</u>ah_

**butter** mantequilla
_mahntay<u>kee</u>lyah_

**buttered** con mantequilla
_kon mahntay<u>kee</u>lyah_

**button** botón _boh<u>ton</u>_

**buy, to** comprar _kohm<u>prahr</u>_

**cabbage** berza _<u>behr</u>tha_;
repollo _ray<u>pohl</u>yoh_

**cake** pastel _pah<u>stayl</u>_;
tarta _<u>tahr</u>tah_

**call up (telephone)** llamada
por teléfono _lyah<u>mahdhah</u>
por tay<u>lay</u>fohnoh_

**call, long-distance**
interurbana
_eentayroor<u>bah</u>nah_

**call, to** llamar _lyah<u>mahr</u>_

**calm** tranquilo _tran<u>kee</u>loh_

**calories** calorías
_kahloh<u>ree</u>ahs_

**camomile** camomila
_kahmoh<u>mee</u>lah_

**can** lata _<u>lah</u>tah_

**can; be able, to** poder
_poh<u>dhayr</u>_

**cancel, to** anular
_ahnoo<u>lahr</u>_; cancelar
_kahnthay<u>lahr</u>_

**candies** dulces _<u>dool</u>thays_

**candle** vela _<u>bay</u>lah_

**candy** caramelo
_kahrah<u>may</u>loh_

**canned meat** carne en lata
_<u>kahr</u>nay ayn <u>lah</u>tah_

**can-opener** abrelatas
_ahbray<u>lah</u>tahs_

**cap, bottle** tapón de la
botella _tah<u>pon</u> day lah
boh<u>tay</u>lyah_

**capers** alcaparras
*ahlkahpahrrahs*
**capon** gallo capado
*gahlyoh kahpahdhoh*
**car park** aparcamiento
*ahpahrkahmyayntoh*
**cardoons** cardos *kahrdohs*
**caretaker** guarda *gwahrdah*
**carrot** zanahoria
*thahnahohryah*
**carry, to** traer/llevar
*trahehr/lyayvar*
**cash desk** caja *kahkhah*
**cash** contado *kohntahdhoh*
**cashier** cajera *cakhayrah*
**casserole dish** cazuela
*kahthwaylah*
**cauliflower** coliflor
*koleeflor*
**celery** apio *ahpyoh*
**center** centro *thayntroh*
**central** central *thayntrahl*
**cereals** cereales
*thayrayahlays*
**chair** silla *seelyah*
**champagne** champán
*shahmpahn*
**change** resto *raystoh*
**change (small)**
monedas/dinero suelto
*mohnaydahs/ deenayroh
swayltoh*

**change, keep the** Tenga, la
vuelta *Tayngah, lah
bwehltah*
**change, to** cambiar
*kahmbyahr*
**charge, to; debit, to** cargar
en cuenta *kahrgahr ayn
kwayntah*
**cheap** barato *bahrahtoh*
**check** cheque *chaykay*
**check, to** controlar
*kohntrohlahr*
**checkout** caja *kahkhah*
**cheese** queso *kaysoh*
**cherry** cereza *thayraythah*
**chestnut** castaña
*kahstahniah*; marrón
*mahrrohn*
**chew, to** masticar
*mahsteekahr*
**chicken** pollo *pohlyoh*
**chick-peas** garbanzos
*gahrbahnthohs*
**chicory** achicoria
*ahcheekohreeah*
**child** niño *neenioh*
**chili pepper** guindilla
*geendeelyah*
**chocolate** chocolate
*chohkohlahtay*
**chocolate, hot** chocolate
líquido *chohkohlahtay
leekeedhoh*

121

**chocolates** chocolatinas
*chohkohlahteenahs;*
bombones *bohmbohnays*

**chop** chuleta *choolaytah*

**chop, to** triturar *treetoorahr*

**chopped** triturado
*treetoorahdhoh*

**Christmas** Navidad
*Nahbeedhadh*

**cigar** puro *pooroh*

**cigarette** cigarrillo
*theekhahrreelyoh*

**cinnamon** canela
*kahnaylah*

**citrus fruits** los agrios *los
ahkhryohs*

**city** ciudad *thyoodhahdh*

**clams** almejas
*ahlmehkhahs*

**clams (small)** chirlas
*cheerlahs*

**clean** limpio *leempyoh*

**clear** claro *klahroh*

**client** cliente *kleeayntay*

**climb, to** subir *soobheer*

**cloakroom** guardarropa
*khwahrdahrrohpah*

**clock** reloj *rehlokh*

**close, to** cerrar *thehrrahr*

**closed** cerrado
*thehrrahdhoh*

**closure** cierre *thyehrray*

**coals** brasa *brahsah*

**coat** abrigo *ahbreegoh*

**cockerel** gallo pequeño
*gahlyoh paykaynioh*

**cocoa** cacao *kahkow*

**coconut** (nueces de) coco
(*nwaythays day*) *kohkoh*

**coffee** café *kahfay*; **black
coffee** café solo *kahfay
sohloh*; **coffee with milk**
café con leche *kahfay kon
laychay*; **decaffeinated
coffee** café descafeinado
*kahfay dayskahfayeenahdoh*;
**espresso coffee** café
expreso *kahfay
exspraysoh*

**coin** moneda *mohnaydah*

**cold** frío *freeoh*

**color** color *kohlor*

**coloring agents** colorantes
*kohlorahntays*

**come back, to** volver
*vohlbayr*

**come out, to** salir *sahleer*

**come, to** venir *bayneer*

**comfortable** cómodo
*kohmohdoh*

**communication**
comunicación
*kohmooneekahthyon*

**complaint** reclamación
*rayklahmahthyon*

**complete** integral
*eentaygrahl*

**compulsory** obligatorio
*ohbhleegahtohryoh*

**cone** cono *kohnoh*

**confirm, to** confirmar
*kohnfeermahr*

**contact lenses** lentillas
*laynteelyahs*

**continue, to** continuar
*conteenooahr*

**control, to** controlar
*kohntrohlahr*

**convenient** cómodo
*kohmohdoh*

**cook** cocinero
*kohtheenayroh*

**cook, to** cocer *kohthayr*

**cooked** cocido *kotheedhoh*

**cooking** coción *cothyon*;
cocina *kohtheenah*

**cool** fresco *frehskoh*

**cool, to** enfriar *aynfreeahr*

**cork** tapón de la botella
*tahpon day lah bohtaylyah*

**corn** maíz *maeeth*

**corner** ángulo *ahngooloh*;
esquina *ayskeenah*

**corn-on-the-cob** mazorca
*mahthohrkah*

**cost** coste *kohstay*

**cost, to** costar *kohstahr*

**cotton** algodón
*ahlkhohdon*

**country** país *payees*

**countryside** campo
*kahmpoh*

**country-style** rústico
*roosteekoh*

**course** plato *plahtoh*

**course, main** manjar
*mahnkhahr*

**cover charge** cubierto
*koobyehrtoh*

**cover** cubierto
*koobyehrtoh*

**cover, to** cubrir *koobreer*

**crab** cangrejo
*kahngrehkhoh*

**cream** crema *kraymah*

**cream/single/whipped**
nata/líquida/montada
*nahtah/leekweedhah/
mohntahdhah*

**credit card** tarjeta de
crédito *tahrkhaytah day
kraydheetoh*

**crêpe** oreja de abad
*oraykha day ahbahd*

**crisp** crujiente
*krookhyayntay*

**croissant** media luna
*maydheeah loonah*

**croquettes** croquetas
*krochaytahs*

**croutons** tostadas
*tohstahdhohs*
**crowded** lleno de gente
*lyaynoh day khayntay*
**crunchy** crujiente
*krookhyayntay*
**crystal** cristal *kreestahl*
**cube (ice-cube)** cubito (de
hielo) *koobheetoh (day
yayloh)*
**cucumber** pepino
*paypeenoh*
**cuisine** cocina *kohtheenah*
**cup, ice-cream** copa
*kohpah*
**cup/(small) coffee cup**
taza/tacita *tahthah/tathita*
**currency** divisa *deebeesah*
**cushion**
almohada/almohadilla
*ahlmohahdhah/
ahlmohahdheelyah*
**customer** cliente
*kleeayntay*
**cut, to** cortar *kohrtahr*
**cutlery** cubiertos
*koobyehrtohs*
**cuttlefish** sepias *saypyahs*

**dance, to** bailar *bighlahr*
**dark** oscuro *ohskooroh*
**date (meeting)** cita *theetah*

**dates (fruit)** dátiles
*dahteelays*
**day** día *deeah*
**December** diciembre
*deethyaymbray*
**decorated** decorado
*daykohrahdhoh*
**decoration** decoración
*daykohrahthyon*
**delay** retraso *raytrahsoh*
**demand** pregunta/petición
*praygoontah/payteethyohn*
**dentures** dentadura postiza
*dayntahdhoorah
pohsteethah*
**depart, to** irse *eersay*
**deposit, to** depositar
*daypohseetahr*
**dessert** postre *pohstray*
**diabetic** diabético
*deeahbayteekoh*
**diet** alimentación
*ahleemayntahthyon*
**diet (slimming)** dieta
*deeaytah*
**different** distinto
*deesteentoh*
**difficult** difícil *deefeetheel*
**digestible** digerible
*deekhayreeblay*
**digestive** digestivo
*deekhaysteeboh*

**dinner** cena _thaynah_

**direction** dirección
  _deerehkthyon_

**directions** indicaciones
  _eendeekahthyonays_

**dirty** sucio _soothyoh_

**disabled** minusválido
  _meenoosbahleedhoh_

**discothèque** discoteca
  _deeskohtaykah_

**dish** plato _plahtoh_

**dish, sundae** copa _kohpah_

**disinfect** desinfectar
  _dayseenfayktahr_

**disinfectant** desinfectante
  _dayseenfayktahntay_

**distance** distancia
  _deestahnthyah_

**distributor** distribuidor
  _deestreebweedohr_

**disturb, to** molestar
  _mohlaystahr_

**do, to** hacer _ahthehr_

**doctor** médico
  _mehdheekoh_

**documents** documentos
  _dokoomayntohs_

**dollars** dólares _dohlahrays_

**door** puerta _pwayrtah_

**double** doble _dohblay_

**down** abajo _ahbhahkhoh_

**drink** bebida _baybheedah_

**drink, to** beber _baybhayr_

**dry** seco _saykoh_

**drumstick** muslo de pollo
  _moosloh day pohlyoh_

**duck** pato _pahtoh_

**dummy** chupete
  _choopaytay_

**each** cada _kahdhah_

**earring** pendiente
  _payndyayntay_

**Easter** Semana Santa
  _Saymahnah Sahntah_

**easy** fácil _fahtheel_

**eat, to** comer _kohmehr_

**economical** barato
  _bahrahtoh_

**EEC** CEE _thay ay ay_

**eel** anguila _ahngweelah_

**egg** huevo _wayvoh_; **boiled
  eggs** huevos duros
  _wayvohs doorohs_; **eggs
  fried in butter** huevos con
  mantequilla _wayvohs kon
  mahntaykeelyah_;
  **scrambled eggs** huevos
  revueltos _wayvohs
  raybwehltohs_

**eggplant** berenjena
  _bayraynkhaynah_

**eggwhite** clara de huevo
  _klahrah day wayvoh_

**elevator** ascensor _ahsthaynsohr_

**embassy** embajada _aymbahkhahdhah_

**empty** vacío _bahthyoh_

**enclosed** incluido _eenklooeedhoh_

**end** fin _feen_

**endive** endivia _ayndeebheeah_

**end-of-the-line (bus, etc.)** terminal de parada _tehrmeenahl day pahrahdhah_

**England** Inglaterra _Eenglahtehrrah_

**English** inglés _eenglays_

**enjoy, to** degustar _daygoostahr_

**enough** bastante _bahstahntay_

**enough, to be** bastar _bahstahr_

**enter, to** entrar _ayntrahr_

**entrance, entry** entrada _ayntradhah_

**envelope** sobre _sohbray_

**equal** igual _eekwahll_

**error** error _ayrrohr_

**evening** tarde noche _tahrday nohchay_

**evening, this** esta noche _aystah nohchay_

**every** cada _kahdhah_

**evil** mal/o _mahl/mahloh_

**except** excepto _exthayptoh_

**exchange rate** cambio _kahmbyoh_

**excursion** excursión _exkoorsyon_

**exit** salida _sahleedhah_

**expense** compra _kohmprah_

**expensive** caro _kahroh_

**experienced** experto _expayrtoh_

**expert** experto _expayrtoh_

**extension, (telephone)** interno _eentayrnoh_

**external** externo _extayrnoh_

**extract** extracto _extrahkhtoh_

**eye** ojo _ohkhoh_

**fainted** desvanecido _desvanezhido_

**fall, to** caerse _kahayrsay_

**familiar** familiar _fahmeelyahr_

**family (adj.)** familiar _fahmeelyahr_

**family** familia _fahmeelyah_

**famous** famoso _fahmohsoh_

**fancy cake** pasta (dulce) _pahstah (doolthay)_

**far** lejos _lehkhos_

**fast** rápido _rahpeedhoh_

**fat** graso/gordo _grahsoh/gohrdhoh_

**favor** favor _fahvor_

**February** febrero _fehbrehroh_

**feet/on foot** pie/a pie _pyay/ah pyay_

**fennel** hinojo _eenohkhoh_

**few, a** algunos _ahlgoonohs_; poco _pohkoh_

**field** campo _kahmpoh_

**fig** higo _eegoh_

**filled** relleno _raylyaynoh_

**fillet** filete _feelaytay_

**filling** relleno _raylyaynoh_

**filter, to** filtrar _feeltrahr_

**find, to** encontrar _aynkohntrahr_

**fine** sutil _sooteel_

**finish, to** terminar _tehrmeenahr_

**fire** fuego _fwaygoh_

**fish** pescado/pez _payskahdhoh/pehth_

**fizzy** espumoso/con mucho gas _ayspoomohsoh/kon moochoh gas_

**flame** llama _lyahmah_

**flask (straw-covered)** botella _bohtaylyah_

**flavor** gusto _goostoh_; sabor _sahbhohr_

**flavor, to** saborear _sahbhohrayahr_

**flavoring** sazón _sahthon_

**flesh** pulpa _poolpah_

**flight** vuelo _bwayloh_

**floor (story)** piso _peesoh_

**flour** harina _ahreenah_

**flowers** flores _flohrays_

**fly** mosca _mohskah_

**for** por/para _por/ pahrah_

**foreign** extranjero _extrahnkhayroh_

**foreigner** extranjero _extrahnkhayroh_

**forget, to** olvidar _ohlbeedhahr_

**fork** tenedor _taynaydhohr_

**forward** adelante _ahdaylahntay_

**fourth** cuarto _kwahrtoh_

**fragrance** aroma _ahrohmah_

**France** Francia _frahnthyah_

**free** gratis _grahtees_; libre _leebray_

**French** francés _franzhès_

**French beans** judías verdes _khoodheeahs behrdays_

**French fries** patatas fritas _pahtahtahs freetahs_

**fresh** fresco _frehskoh_

**Friday** viernes _byayr_nays
**fried food** fritura free_too_rah
**fried/mixed fry** frito/fritura
  mixta _free_toh/free_too_rah
  _mee_xtah
**friend** amigo ah_mee_goh
**front, in** delante
  day_lahn_tay
**frozen** congelado
  kohnkhay_lah_dhoh
**fruit juice, freshly squeezed**
  zumo natural _thoo_moh
  nah_too_rahl
**fruit salad** macedonia
  mahthay_doh_nyah
**fruit/fresh/dried**
  fruta/fresca/seca
  _froo_tah/_freh_skah/_say_kah
**frying pan** sartén sahr_tayn
**fry-up** fritura free_too_rah
**full** lleno _lyay_noh
**full-bodied** corposo
  kohr_poh_soh

**game (pheasant, etc.)** caza
  _kah_thah
**garden** jardín khahr_deen
**garlic** ajo _ah_khoh
**garnish** guarnición
  gwahrnee_thyon
**gelatine** gelatina
  khaylah_tee_nah

**gender** género _khay_nayroh
**genuine** auténtico
  owtayn_tee_koh
**Germany** Alemania
  Ahlay_mah_nyah
**get on, to** subir soo_bheer
**gherkins** pepinillos
  paypec_nee_lyohs
**giblets** asaduras
  ahsah_doo_rahs
**girl** chica _chee_kah
**give, to** dar dahr
**glass** cristal kree_stahl
**glass/liqueur glass** vaso / v.
  pequeño _bah_soh / b.
  pay_kay_nioh
**glasses** gafas _gah_fahs
**gloves** guantes _gwahn_tays
**go, to** ir eer
**go back, to** volver vohl_bayr
**go out, to** salir sah_leer
**go up, to** subir soo_bheer
**gold** oro _oh_roh
**golden brown** dorado
  doh_rah_dhoh
**good** bien _byayn;_ bueno
  _bway_noh
**goose** oca _oh_kah
**gourd** calabaza
  kahlah_bha_thah
**grain** grano _grah_noh

**grapefruit** pomelo
*pohmayloh*

**grapes** uvas *oovahs*

**grated** rallado *rahlyahdhoh*

**gratin, (au)** gratinado
*grahteenahdhoh*

**gravy** guiso *gweesoh*

**greasy** untado/grasiento
*oontahdhoh/grahsyayntoh*

**great** grande *grahnday*

**Great Britain** Gran Bretaña
*Grahn Braytahniah*

**green** verde *behrday*

**grill** parrilla *pahrreelyah*

**group** grupo *groopoh*;
pandilla *pahndeelyah*

**guard** guarda *gwahrdah*

**guide** guía *gweeah*

**Guinea fowl** gallina de
Guinea *gahlyeenah day
Geenayah*

**hake** merluza *mayrloothah*

**half** mitad/medio
*meetahdh/maydhyoh*

**hall** sala *sahlah*

**ham** jamón *khahmon*

**hand** mano *mahnoh*

**handbag** bolso pequeño
*bolsoh paykaynioh*

**happen, to** suceder
*soothaydayr*

**happened, what (has)** qué
ha pasado *kay ah
pahsahdhoh*

**happy** contento
*kohntayntoh*

**hard** duro *dooroh*

**hare** liebre *lyehbray*

**harmless** inocuo *eenokwoh*

**hat** sombrero *sohmbrayroh*

**have a good meal!** ¡qué
aproveche! *kay
ahprohbaychay*

**have to, to** deber *daybhayr*

**hazelnuts** avellanas
*ahvaylyahnahs*

**headache** dolor de cabeza
*dohlor day kahbhaythah*

**hear, to** oír *oheer*

**heat, to** calentar
*kahlayntahr*

**heating** calefacción
*kahlayfahkthyon*

**heavy** pesado *paysahdhoh*

**hello (answering phone)**
diga *deegah*

**help, to** ayudar *ahyoodhar*

**hen** gallina *gahlynah*

**herb tea** tisana *teesahnah*

**herbs, aromatic** hierbas
aromáticas *yehrbahs
ahrohmahteekahs*

**here** aquí *ahkee*

**herring** arenque *ahrehnkay*
**high chair** silla para bebés
 *seelyah pahrah baybays*
**hire, to** alquilar *ahlkeelahr*
**hold, to** tener *taynayr*
**holiday, public** fiesta
 *fyaystah*
**holidays** vacaciones
 *bahkahthyohnays*
**honey** miel *myehl*
**hors-d'oeuvres** entremés
 *ayntraymays*
**hospital** hospital
 *ohspeetahl*
**hot** caliente *kahlyayntay*
**hot (spicy)** picante
 *peekahntay*
**hotel** hotel *ohtayl*
**hour** hora *ohrah*
**how** como *kohmoh*
**how many** cuantos
 *kwahntohs*
**how much** cuanto
 *kwahntoh*
**hundred** cien/to *thyayn/toh*
**hunger** hambre *ahmbray*
**hurry** prisa *preesah*
**hurry, to be in a** tener prisa
 *taynayr preesah*
**hurry, to do something in a**
 apresurarse
 *ahpraysoorahrsay*

**husband** marido
 *mahreedhoh*

**ice** hielo *yayloh,*
**ice-cream** helado
 *aylahdhoh*
**ice-cream shop (parlor)**
 heladería *aylahdhayreeah*
**identity card** carnet de
 identidad *kahrnay day
 eedaynteedhad*
**ill** enfermo *aynfehrmoh*
**important** importante
 *eempohrtahntay*
**impossible** imposible
 *eempohseebhlay*
**in cash** al contado *ahl
 kohntahdhoh*
**in order to** por/para *pohr/
 pahrah*
**included, inclusive** incluído
 *eenklooeedhoh;*
 comprendido
 *kohmprayndeedhoh*
**inconvenient** incómodo
 *eenkohmohdhoh*
**indoors** al cubierto *ahl
 koobyehrtoh*
**inexpensive** barato
 *bahrahtoh*
**inform, to** advertir
 *ahdbehrteer;* informar
 *eenformahr*

**information** informaciones
  *eenformahthyonays*
**inn** tasca *tahskah*
**insect** insecto *eensehktoh*
**inside** dentro de *dayntroh
  day*; interno *eentayrnoh*
**instead** en cambio *ayn
  kahmbyoh*
**internal** interno *eentayrnoh*
**invite, to** invitar *eenbeetahr*
**invoice** factura *fahktoorah*
**Ireland** Irlanda *Eerlahndah*
**Italy** Italia *Eetahlyah*

**jacket** chaqueta
  *chahkaytah*
**jam** confitura
  *kohnfeetoorah*; mermelada
  *mayrmaylahdah*
**January** enero *aynayroh*
**jelly** gelatina
  *khaylahteenah*
**jug** jarra *khahrrah*
**juice** zumo *thoomoh*
**July** julio *khoolyoh*
**June** junio *khoonyoh*
**just** propio *prohpyoh*

**keep, to** custodiar/cuidar
  *koostohdyar/kweedahr*;
  tener *taynayr*
**keeper** guarda *gwahrdah*

**kid (young goat)** cabra
  pequeña *kahbrah
  paykayniah*
**kidney** riñón *reeniohn*
**kind (type)** género
  *khaynayroh*
**kitchen** cocina *kohtheenah*
**knife** cuchillo *koocheelyoh*
**know, to** saber *sahbhayr*

**label** etiqueta *ayteekaytah*
**lady** señora *sayniohrah*
**lager** c. clara *c. klahrah*
**lake** lago *laghoh*
**lamb** carnero *kahrnayroh*
**lamb** cordero *kohrdayroh*
**lard** manteca de cerdo
  *mahntaykah day thehrdoh*
**lard** tocino *tohtheenoh*
**large** grande *grahnday*
**last** último *oolteemoh*
**lean** delgado/sin grasa
  *daylhahdhoh/seen grahsah*
**leave, to** dejar *dehkhahr*;
  irse *eersay*
**leave, to** salir *sahleer*
**leeks** puerros *pwayrrohs*
**left, to be** quedar/se
  *kaydahr/say*
**leg** pierna *pyehrnah*
**lemon** limón *leemon*

**lemonade** limonada
  *leemohnahdah*
**lens** lente *layntay*
**lentils** lentejas *layntaykhas*
**less** menos *maynohs*
**lettuce** lechuga *laychoogah*
**lift** ascensor *ahsthaynsohr*
**light** ligero *leekhayroh*
**light** luz *looth*
**light, to** encender
  *aynthayndhayr*
**like** como *kohmoh*
**line** hilo *eeloh*
**line (telephone)** línea
  *leenayah*
**liqueur** licor *leekor*
**list** lista *leestah*
**lit** encendido
  *aynthayndeedhoh*
**liter** litro *leetroh*
**little** poco *pohkoh*
**liver/livers** hígado/
  higaditos *eekhahdhoh/
  eekhadheetohs*
**lobster** langosta
  *lahngohstah*
**lobster (baby)** langostino
  *lahngohsteenoh*
**local** local *lohkahl*
**loin** lomo *lohmoh*
**long** largo *lahrgoh*

**look at, to** mirar *meerahr*
**lose, to** perder *pehrdhayr*
**lounge** sala *sahlah*
**lunch** comida *kohmeedhah*

**mackerel** caballa
  *kahbhahlyah*
**macrobiotic** macrobiótico
  *mahkrohbeeohteekoh*
**Madam** señora *sayniohrah*
**maize** maíz *maeeth*
**make, to** hacer *ahthehr*
**management** dirección
  *deerehkthyon*
**manager** director
  *deerayktohr*
**manner** modo *mohdhoh*
**many** mucho *moochoh*
**March** marzo *mahrthoh*
**marinade** escabechada
  *ayskahbhaychahdah*
**market** mercado
  *mehrkahdhoh*
**marmalade** mermelada
  *mayrmaylahdah*
**marrow** calabaza
  *kahlahbhathah*
**match** cerilla *thehreelyah*
**mature** estacionado
  *aystahthyonahdhoh*;
  maduro *mahdooroh*
**May** mayo *mahyoh*

**mayonnaise** mayonesa
*mighohnaysah*
**meal** comida *kohmeedhah*
**mean, to/** significar
*seegneefeekahr*
**mean, what does it?** ¿qué
significa? *kay
seegneefeekah*
**meat** carne *kahrnay*
**meatballs** albóndigas
*ahlbhohndeekhahs*
**medicine** medicina
*maydheethynah*
**meet, to** encontrar
*aynkohntrahr*
**melon** melón *maylon*
**mention it, don't** de nada
*day nahdhah*
**menu** menú *maynoo*
**message** comunicación
*kohmooneekahthyon*
**mild** dulce *doolthay*
**milk** leche *laychay*
**mince, to** triturar
*treetoorahr*
**minced** triturado
*treetoorahdhoh*
**minced meat** carne triturada
*kahrnay treetoorahdhah*
**mineral water** agua mineral
*ahgwah meenayrahl*
**mint** menta *mayntah*

**minus** menos *maynohs*
**minute** minuto *meenootoh*
**Miss** señorita *sayniohreetah*
**mistake** equivocación
*aykeevohkahthyon*
**misunderstanding**
malentendido
*mahlayntayndeedhoh*
**mixed** mixto *meextoh*
**mixture** mezcla *maythklah*
**Monday** lunes *loonays*
**month** mes *mays*
**monuments** monumentos
*mohnoomayntohs*
**more** más *mahs*
**morning** mañana
*mahniahnah*
**mosquito** mosquitos
*mohskeetohs*
**mother** madre *mahdray*
**mount, to** subir *soobheer*
**mouth** boca *bohkah*
**Mrs.** señora *sayniohrah*
**much** mucho *moochoh*
**much, not** poco *pohkoh*
**mullet** róbalo *rohbahloh*
**mullet, red** salmonetes
*sahlmohnaytays*
**museum** museo *moosayoh*
**mushrooms/fresh/dried**
setas/frescas/secas
*saytahs/frehskahs/saykahs*

**music** música _mooseekah_

**mussels** mejillones _mehkheelyohnays_

**must** deber _daybhayr_

**mustard** mostaza _mohstahthah_

**mutton** carnero _kahrnayroh_

**name** nombre _nohmbray_

**napkin** servilleta _sehrbeelyaytah_

**narrow** estrecho _aystraychoh_

**nearly** casi _kahsee_

**need** necesidad _naythayseedhahdh_

**need of, to have** necesitar _naythayseetahr_

**neighborhood** alrededores _ahlraydhaydhohrays_

**never** nunca _noonkah_

**New Year's Eve** Nochevieja _Nohchaybyaykhah_

**newspaper** periódico _payryodheekoh_

**no** no/ninguno/a _noh/neengoonoh/ah_

**nobody** nadie _nahdyay_

**noise** ruido _rweedhoh_

**noisy** ruidoso _rweedhohsoh_

**non-alcoholic, alcohol-free** sin alcohol _seen ahlkohohl_

**none** ninguno/a _neengoonoh/ah_

**non-smoker** no fumador _noh foomahdhohr_

**noodles** fideos finos _feedhayohs feenohs_

**no-one** nadie _nahdyay_

**north** norte _nortay_

**nothing** nada _nahdhah_

**November** noviembre _nohvyaymbray_

**number** número _noomayroh_

**nutcracker** cascanueces _kaskahnwaythays_

**nutmeg** nuez moscada _nooayth moskahdah_

**nutrition** alimentación _ahleemayntahthyon_

**oat** avena _ahbaynah_

**obligatory** obligatorio _ohbhleegahtohryoh_

**obtain, to** obtener _obtehnayr_

**October** octubre _oktoobray_

**octopus** pulpo _poolpoh_

**offal** asaduras _ahsahdoorahs_

**often** a menudo _ah maynoodhoh_

**oil** aceite _athaytay_

**oil cruet** aceitera
  *athaytayrah*

**oil, in** en aceite *ayn*
  *athaytay*

**oily** untado/grasiento
  *oontahdhoh/grahsayntoh*

**old** viejo *byaykhoh*

**olive** aceitunas
  *ahthaytoonahs*

**omelette** tortilla *torteelyah*

**on (prep.)** encima
  *aynthymah*

**on** encendido
  *aynthayndeedhoh*

**onion** cebolla *thaybohlyah*

**only** solamente
  *sohlahmayntay*; sólo
  *sohloh*

**open** abierto *ahbhyehrtoh*

**operate, to** funcionar
  *foonthyonahr*

**orange** naranja
  *nahrahnkhah*

**orangeade** naranjada
  *nahrahnkhahdhah*

**order** peticion *payteethyon*

**order, to** ordenar/pedir
  *ohrdaynahr/ pehdheer*

**oregano** orégano
  *ohraygahnoh*

**original** auténtico
  *owtaynteekoh*

**other** otro *ohtroh*

**out of order**
  estropeado/destrozo
  *aystrohpayahdhoh/*
  *daystrohthoh*

**outside** externo *extayrnoh*;
  al aire libre *ahl ighray*
  *leebray*; fuera *fwayrah*

**oven** horno *ohrnoh*

**overseas** extranjero
  *extrahnkhayroh*

**own** propio *prohpyoh*

**ox** buey *bway*

**oysters** ostras *ohstrahs*

**pacifier** chupete
  *choopaytay*

**packaged** confeccionado
  *kohnfaykthyonahdhoh*

**pain** mal/dolor *mahl/*
  *dohlor*

**pair** par *pahr*

**pancake** oreja de abad
  *oraykha day ahbahd*

**paper** papel *pahpehl*

**paper tissue** pañuelo de
  papel *pahniwaylohs day*
  *pahpehl*

**papers (passport, etc.)**
  documentos
  *dohkoomayntohs*

**parents** padres *pahdrays*

**park** parque *pahrkay*

**parking lot** aparcamiento
  ahpahr_kahmyayn_toh
**parsley** perejil payray_kheel_
**part** parte _pahr_tay
**party** fiesta _fyays_tah
**party (of people)** pandilla
  pahn_deel_yah
**passport** pasaporte
  pahsah_por_tay
**pasta** pasta _pahs_tah
**pastry shop** pastelería
  pahstaylay_ree_ah
**pastry, short** pastaflora
  pahstah_floh_rah
**pay** pagar pah_gahr_
**payment** pago _pahk_hoh
**peach** melocotón
  maylohkoh_ton_
**peanut** cacahuete
  kahkah_way_tay
**pear** pera _peh_rah
**peas** guisantes
  gwee_sahn_tays
**peel, to** pelar pay_lahr_
**pen** bolígrafo boh_lee_grafoh
**pencil** lápiz lah_peeth_
**pepper** pimienta
  pee_myayn_tah
**pepper mill** triturador de
  pimienta treetoorah_dhohr_
  day pee_myayn_tah
**per** por/para _por_/ pahrah

**perch** perca _pehr_kah
**performance** espectáculo
  ayspehk_tah_kooloh
**perhaps** quizás kee_thahs_
**permission** permitido
  pehrmee_teed_hoh
**permit** permitido
  pehrmee_teed_hoh
**persimmon** caqui _kah_kee
**petit four** pasta (dulce)
  _pahs_tah (_dool_thay)
**pharmacy** farmacia
  far_mah_thyah
**pheasant** faisán fahee_sahn_
**phone call** llamada
  telefónica lyah_mahdh_ah
  taylay_foh_neekah
**photograph** fotografía
  fohtohgrah_fee_ah
**pickled** en vinagre ayn
  bee_nah_gray
**pie** pastel pah_stayl_; tarta
  _tahr_tah
**pig** suino _swee_noh; cerdo
  _thehr_doh
**pigeon** pichón pee_chohn_
**pike** lucio _looth_yoh
**pill** pastilla pah_steel_yah;
  píldora _peel_dohrah
**pillow** almohada/
  almohadilla ahlmoh_ahdh_ah/
  ahlmohah_dheel_yah

**pine nuts** piñones
*peeniohnays*

**pineapple** piña *peeniah*

**pistachio nuts** pistachos
*peestahchohs*

**place** lugar *loogahr*; sitio
*seetyoh*; local *lohkahl*

**place, to** meter/poner
*maytayr/pohnayr*

**plain (without sauce, etc.)**
sin salsa *seen sahlsah*

**plate** plato *plahtoh*

**play, to** jugar *khoogahr*

**please** por favor *por fahvor*

**please, to** placer *plahthehr*

**pluck, to** pelar *paylahr*

**plums** ciruelas
*theerwaylahs*

**poisoning** intoxicación
*eentoxykahthyon*

**popsicle** polo *pohloh*

**pork** suido *sweedoh*;
cerdo *thehrdoh*

**portion** porción *porthyon*

**possible** posible
*pohseebhlay*

**postcard** postal *pohstahl*

**potatoes/boiled/roast**
patatas/cocidas/asadas
*pahtahtahs/kohthydhahs/
asahdhahs*

**power supply** corriente
*korryayntay*

**prefer, to** preferir
*prayfehreer*

**pregnant** embarazada
*ehmbahrathahdhah*

**prepare, to** preparar
*praypahrahr*

**preserved** conservado
*kohnsayrbahdoh*

**presevatives** conservantes
*kohnsayrbahntays*

**price** precio *praythyoh*

**pulp** pulpa *poolpah*

**pumpkin** calabaza
*kahlahbhathah*

**purée** puré *pooray*

**put out, to** apagar
*ahpahkhahr*

**put, to** meter/poner
*maytayr/pohnayr*

**quail** codorniz
*kohdohrneeth*

**quarter** cuarto *kwahrtoh*

**question** pregunta/petición
*praygoontah/payteethyohn*

**quick** rápido *rahpeedhoh*

**quickly** rápidamente
*rahpeedhahmayntay*

**rabbit** conejo *kohnaykhoh*

**radio** radio *rahdhyoh*

**radishes** rábanos
*rahbhahnohs*

**raincoat** impermeable
*eempehrmayahblay*

**raisins** uvas pasas *oovahs
pahsahs*

**raspberries** fresones
*fraysohnays*

**raw vegetables** crudeza
*kroodhethah*

**raw** crudo *kroodhoh*

**read, to** leer *lehayr*

**ready-made** confeccionado
*kohnfaykthyonahdhoh*

**really** propio *prohpyoh*

**receipt** recibo *raytheebhoh*

**recipe** receta *raythaytah*

**red** rojo *rohkhoh*

**redcurrant** grosella
*grohsaylyah*

**refrigerator** frigorífico
*freegohreefeekoh*

**refund** reembolso
*rayehmbohlsoh*

**region** región *raykhyohn*

**remain, to** quedarse
*kaydahr/say*

**remove, to** quitar *keetahr*

**rent, to** alquilar *ahlkeelahr*

**reply, to** responder
*rayspohndayr*

**reserve, to** reservar
*rehsayrbahr*

**reserved** reservado
*rehsehrbahdhoh*

**restaurant** restaurante
*raystowrahntay*

**return** regreso *raygraysoh*

**return, to** volver *vohlbayr*

**ribs** costillas *kohsteelyahs*

**rice** arroz *ahrroth*

**right/on the right** derecha/a
la derecha *dayraychah/ah
lah dayraychah*

**ripe** estacionado
*aystahthyonahdhoh*;
maduro *mahdooroh*

**road** calle/carreterra
*kahlyay/kahrraytayrah*

**roast** asado *ahsahdhoh*

**roasted** asado *ahsahdhoh*

**roll (filled)** bocadillo
*bohkahdheelyoh*

**room (hotel)** habitación
*ahbheetahthyon*

**room** sala *sahlah*

**rosemary** romero
*rohmayroh*

**rural** rústico *roosteekoh*

**safety pin** broche de
seguridad *brohchay day
saykhooreedhadh*

**saffron** azafrán *ahtahfrahn*

**sage** salvia *sahlbyah*

**salad** ensalada
aynsah*lah*dhah
**salmon, smoked** salmón
ahumado sah*lmon*
ahoo*mah*dhoh
**salt** sal sahl
**salt shaker** salero sah*lay*roh
**salted** salado sah*lah*dhoh
**salty** salado sah*lah*dhoh
**same** mismo *mees*moh
**sardine** sardinas
sahr*dee*nahs
**Saturday** sábado
*sah*bhadhoh
**sauce** salsa *sahl*sah
**saucepan** cazuela
kahth*way*lah
**saucepan** sartén sahr*tayn*
**sausage** salchicha
sahl*chee*chah
**sausages** embutidos
aymboo*teed*hohs
**savory** salado sah*lah*dhoh
**say, to** decir day*theer*
**schedule** horario oh*rah*ryoh
**sea** mar mahr
**seafood** mariscos
mah*ree*skohs
**season** estación/ temporada
aystah*thyon*
/taympoh*rah*dhah
**season, to** saborear
sahbhohray*ahr*

**seasoning** sazón sah*thon*
**second** segundo
say*khoon*doh
**sedative** calmante
kahl*mahn*tayh
**see, to** ver behr
**self** mismo *mees*moh
**sell, to** vender bayn*dayr*
**September** septiembre
sehp*tyaym*bray
**service** servicio
sehr*beeth*yoh
**service charge** servicio
sehr*beeth*yoh
**serviette** servilleta
sehrbee*lyay*tah
**set the table, to** poner la
mesa poh*nayr* lah *may*sah
**shake, (milk)** batido
bah*teed*hoh
**sharp** ácido *ah*theedhoh
**shell** cáscara *kahs*kahrah
**shell** concha *kon*thyah
**shellfish** crustáceos
kroos*tah*thayohs
**shellfish** moluscos
moh*loos*kohs
**shirt** camisa kah*mee*sah
**shop** tienda *tyayn*dah
**shopping, to go** ir de
compras eer day
*kohm*prahs

**short pastry** pasta flora
*pahstah flohrah*

**shoulder** hombro *ohmbroh*

**show** espectáculo
*ayspehktahkooloh*

**show, to** mostrar *mohstrahr*

**shrimps** gambas *gahmbahs*

**shut** cerrado *thehrrahdhoh*

**sick** enfermo *aynfehrmoh*

**side dish** contorno
*kohntohrnoh*

**side dish** guarnición
*gwahrneethyon*

**sight** vista *beestah*

**signature** firma *feermah*

**simple** simple *seemplay*

**site** sitio *seetyoh*

**skewer, wooden** palillo
*pahleelyoh*

**skewers** broquetas
*brohkaytahs*

**slice** rebanada/ loncha
*raybhahnahdhah/lohnchah*

**sliced** cortado en rebanadas
*kohrtahdhoh ayn
raybhahnahdhahs*

**sliced cold cuts** embutidos
*aymbooteedhohs*

**slowly** despacio
*dayspahthyoh*

**small** pequeño *paykaynioh*

**smell** olor *ohlohr*

**smoked** ahumado
*ahoomahdhoh*

**smoker** fumador
*foomahdhohr*

**smooth** liso *leesoh*

**snack** merienda
*mayryayndah*

**snack** tapa *tahpah*

**snails** caracoles
*kahrahkohlays*

**soap** jabón *khahbhon*

**sole** lenguado
*layngwahdhoh*

**some** algún *ahlgoon*

**some** algunos *ahlgoonohs*

**someone** alguien *ahlgyayn*;
algún/o *ahlgoon/oh*

**something** algo *ahlgoh*

**son** hijo *eekhoh*

**song** canción *kahnthyon*

**sorbet, sherbet** sorbete
*sohrbaytay*

**sort** género *khaynayroh*

**soup** caldo *kahldhoh*

**soup** sopa *sohpah*

**sour** áspero *ahspayroh*;
agrio *ahgryoh*

**south** sur *soor*

**soya** soja *sohkhah*

**sparkling** espumoso/con
mucho gas
*ayspoomohsoh/kon
moochoh gas*

**sparkling mineral water** agua con gas _ahgwah kon gas_

**spices** especias _ayspaythyahs_

**spicy** picante _peekahntay_

**spinach** espinacas _ayspeenahkahs_

**spirits, (high-proof)** superalcohólicos _superalcolicos_

**spit** asador _ahsahdhohr_

**spoon/teaspoon** cuchara/cucharilla _koochahrah/koochahree koochareelyah_

**spring lamb** cordero _kohrdayroh_

**square** plaza _plahthah_

**squid** calamares _kahlahmahrays_

**stairs** escaleras _ayskahlayrahs_

**stamp** sello _saylyoh_

**start** inicio _eeneethyoh_

**station** estación _aystahthyon_

**stay, to** quedarse _kaydahr/say_

**steak** bistec _beestayk_

**steak, grilled** bistec a la plancha _beestayk ah lah plahnchah_

**steamed** al vapor _ahl bapor_

**stew** carne a trozos/estofada _kahrnay ah trohthohs /aystohfahdhah_

**stew** estofado _aystohfahdhoh_

**still** todavía _tohdhahveeah_

**stomachache** dolor de estómago _dohlor day aystohmahgoh_

**stop (bus, train, etc.)** parada _pahrahdhah_

**stop, to** parar _pahrahr_

**stop, to (cease)** dejar _dehkhahr_

**stout** c. oscura _c. ohskoorah_

**straight (drink)** liso _leesoh_

**straight away** enseguida _aynsaygweedah_

**straight on** derecho _dayraychoh_

**strawberry** fresa _fraysah_

**street** calle/carreterra _kahlyay/kahrraytayrah_

**strong** fuerte _fwehrtay_

**stuffed** relleno _raylyaynoh_

**stuffed** relleno _raylyaynoh_

**subtle** sutil _sooteel_

**subway** metro _mehtroh_

**sugar** azúcar _ahthookahr_

**sugar bowl** azucarero
 *ahthookarayroh*
**suitcase** maleta *mahlaytah*
**summer** verano *bayrahnoh*
**summer (adj.)** veraniego /
 de verano
 *behrahnyaygoh/day*
 *bayrahnoh*
**Sunday** domingo
 *dohmeengoh*
**surname** apellido
 *ahpaylyeedhoh*
**surroundings** alrededores
 *ahlraydhaydhohrays*
**sweet** caramelo
 *kahrahmayloh*
**sweet** dulce *doolthay*
**sweet-and-sour** agridulce
 *ahkhreedoolthay*
**sweetener** dulcificante
 *doolthyfeekahntay*
**sweets** dulces *doolthays*
**swim, to** nadar *nahdhahr*
**swimming pool** piscina
 *peestheenah*
**Switzerland** Suiza
 *Sweethah*
**swordfish** pez espada
 *pehth ayspahdhah*
**syrup (in)** (de) jarabe *(day)*
 *kharahbhay*

**table** mesa *maysah*
**tablecloth** mantel *mahntayl*
**take, to** coger/tomar
 *kohkhehr/tohmahr*
**talcum powder** polvos de
 talco *poalbohs day*
 *tahlkoh*
**tangerine** mandarina
 *mahndahreenah*
**tart** pastel *pahstayl*
**tart** tarta *tahrtah*
**tart** agrio *ahkhryoh*
**tart** torta, pastel glaseado
 *tortah, pahstehl*
 *glaysayahdhoh*
**taste** degustación
 *daygoostahthyon*
**taste** gusto *goostoh*
**taste** sabor *sahbhohr*
**taste, to** degustar
 *daygoostahr*
**taste, to** probar/ catar
 *provahr /kahtahr*
**tasting** degustación
 *daygoostahthyon*
**tavern** bodega *bodhaygah*
**tavern** tasca *tahskah*
**tea** té *tay*
**tea cake** pasta (dulce)
 *pahstah (doolthay)*
**telephone** teléfono
 *taylayfohnoh*

**telephone directory** guía
telefónica _gweeah
taylayfohneekah_

**temperature** temperatura
_taympayrahtoorah_

**temperature, room**
temperatura del tiempo
_taympayrahtoorah dayl
tyaympoh_

**tender** blando _blahndhoh_

**terminus** terminal de parada
_tehrmeenahl day
pahrahdhah_

**terrace** terraza _tayrathah_

**thank you** gracias
_grahthyahs_

**thank, to** agradecer
_ahgrahdhaythayr_

**that** ese/aquel _aysah/ahkayl_

**that** que _kay_

**then** después _dayspways_

**thin** delgado/sin grasa
_daylhahdhoh/seen grahsah_

**thin** sutil _sooteel_

**thirst** sed _saydh_

**this** este _aystay_

**thousand** mil _meel_

**thread** hilo _eeloh_

**throat** garganta
_gahrgahntah_

**throw away, to** tirar _teerahr_

**Thursday** jueves
_khwayvays_

**thyme** tomillo _tohmeelyoh_

**ticket** billete _beelyaytay_

**tie** corbata _korbahtah_

**tight** estrecho _aystraychoh_

**time** tiempo _tyaympoh_

**timetable** horario _ohrahryoh_

**tin** lata _lahtah_

**tip** propina _prohpeenah_

**to have** tener _taynayr_

**toast (with glasses)** brindis
_breendees_

**toasted** tostado
_tohstahdhoh_

**toasted** tostado
_tohstahdhoh_

**tobacconist's** estanco
_ehstahnkoh_

**today** hoy _oy_

**together** juntos/as
_khoontohs/ahs_

**toilet** baño _bahnioh_

**toilet, restroom** baño
_bahnioh_

**tomato** tomate _tohmahtay_

**tomorrow** mañana
_mahniahnah_

**tongue** lengua _layngwah_

**too** demasiado
_daymahsyahdhoh_

**too much** demasiado
_daymahsyahdhoh_

**toothpick** palillo
_pahleelyoh_

**tour** vuelta _bwehltah_

**toward(s)** hacia _ahthyah_

**towel** toalla _tohahlyah_

**train** tren _trayn_

**transport/means of t.** transporte, medios de transporte _trahnspohrtay/maydhyohs day t._

**tray** bandeja _bandaykhah_

**trip** excursión _exkoorsyon_

**tripe** callos _kahlyohs_

**trout** trucha _troochah_

**truffle** trufa _troofah_

**try, to** probar _provahr_

**Tuesday** martes _mahrtays_

**tuna** atún _ahtoon_

**turbot** rombo _rohmboh_

**tureen** tarrina _tahrreenah_

**turkey** pavo _pahvoh_

**turn** vuelta _bwehltah_

**turn off, to** apagar _ahpahkhahr_

**turn on, to** encender _aynthayndhayr_

**turn, to** dar vueltas _dahr bwehltahs_

**type** género _khaynayroh_

**ugly** feo _fehoh_

**umbrella** paraguas _pahrahgwahs_

**uncap, to** destapar _daystahpahr_

**uncomfortable** incómodo _eenkohmohdhoh_

**uncork, to** destapar _daystahpahr_

**under** debajo _daybhahkhoh_

**underground (train)** metro _mehtroh_

**understand, to** entender _ayntayndhayr_

**United States** Estados Unidos _Aystahdhohs Ooneedhohs_

**until** hasta _ahstah_

**use, to** usar _oosahr_

**vacant** libre _leebray_

**vacation** vacaciones _bahkahthyohnays_

**vacation** vacaciones _bhahkahtheebhnays_

**vanilla** vainilla _bighneelyah_

**veal** ternero/a _tehrnayroh/ah_

**vegetables** hortalizas _ohrtahlythahs_

**vegetables** verdura _bayrdoorah_

**vegetables** legumbres _laygoombrays_

**vegetarian** vegetariano _baykhaytahryahnoh_

**vending machine**
distribuidor
*deestreebweedohr*

**very** muy *mwee*

**village** pueblo *pwaybloh*

**vinegar** vinagre *beenahgray*

**vintage (year)** temporada
*taympohrahdhah*

**vitamins** vitaminas
*beetahmeenahs*

**wait, to** esperar *ayspayrahr*

**waiter/waitress** camarero/a
*kahmahrayroh/ah*

**walk, to** caminar
*kahmeenahr*

**wall** pared/ muro
*pahrayd/mooroh*

**wallet** cartera *kahrtayrah*

**walnuts** nueces *nwaythays*

**want, to** querer *kayrayr*

**warm, to** calentar
*kahlayntahr*

**warn, to** advertir
*ahdbehrteer*

**wash, to** lavar *labhar*

**wasp** avispa *ahbeespah*

**watch** reloj *rehlokh*

**watermelon** sandía
*sahndeeah*

**water** agua *ahgwah*

**waterproof** impermeable
*eempehrmayahblay*

**way** modo *mohdhoh*

**weak** débil *daybheel*

**Wednesday** miércoles
*myayrkohlays*

**week** semana s*aymahnah*

**weekday** diario *deeahreeoh*

**welcome** bienvenido /a
*beeaynbayneedhoh/ah*

**welcome, you're** de nada
*day nahdhah*

**well** bien *byayn*

**what** cual *kwahl*

**what?** ¿qué? *kay*

**whatever** cualquier/ a
*kwahlkyehr/ah*

**when** cuando *kwahndoh*

**where** donde *dohnday*

**whereas** mientras
*meeayntrahs*

**which** cual *kwahl*

**which one** cual *kwahl*

**while** mientras
*meeayntrahs*

**whip up, to** batir *bahteer*

**white** blanco *blahnkoh*

**whiting** pescadilla
*peskahdheelyah*

**who** quien *kyayn*

**whole** entero *ayntayroh*

**wholemeal** integral
*eentaygrahl*

**why** porque *porkay*
**wife** mujer *mookhehr*
**wild berries** frutos
  selváticos *frootohs*
  *saylbahteekohs*
**window** ventana
  *behntahnah*
**wine** vino *beenoh*; **full-
  bodied w.** v. fuerte, v. de
  cuerpo *b. fwehrtay, b.
  kwehrpoh*; **light w.** v.
  ligero *b. leekhayroh*; **old
  (good quality) w.** v. de
  solera *b. day sohlayrah*;
  **red w.** v. tinto *b. teentoh*;
  **rosé w.** v. rosé/rosado *b.
  rosay/rohsahdhoh*; **white
  w.** v. blanco *b. blahnkoh*
**wine cellar** bodega
  *bodhaygah*
**wineshop** bodega
  *bodhaygah*
**winter** invierno
  *eenbyayrnoh*
**wire** hilo *eeloh*
**with** con *kon*

**without** sin *seen*
**woman** mujer *mookhehr*
**word** palabra *pahlahbrah*
**work** trabajo *trahbhahkhoh*
**work, to (machine, etc.)**
  funcionar *foonthyonahr*
**wrapped-up** confeccionado
  *kohnfaykthyonahdhoh*
**write, to** escribir
  ayskreebheer

**year** año *ahnioh*
**yeast** levadura
  *laybahdoorah*
**yellow** amarillo
  *ahmahreelyoh*
**yesterday** ayer *ighehr*
**yet** todavía *tohdhahveeah*
**yolk** yema *yaymah*
**young** joven *khohvehn*
**young woman** señorita
  *sayniohreetah*

**zucchini** calabacines
  *kahlahbhatheenays*

**abajá de Algeciras** see
"Regional Dishes" page 37

**abajo** down

**abierto** open

**abrebotellas** bottle opener

**abrelatas** can opener

**abrigo** overcoat

**abril** April

**aceite** oil

**aceitera** oil cruet

**aceitunas** olives

**acelgas** chard

**aceptar con agrado** to
appreciate; to accept with
pleasure

**achicoria** chicory

**ácido** acid

**adelante** forward

**aditivo** additive

**adulto** adult

**advertir** to point out; to
notify; to inform; to warn

**aeropuerto** airport

**afuega'l pitu** see "Cheeses",
page 8

**agosto** August

**agradecer** to thank

**agridulce** sweet-and-sour

**agridulce, al** see
"Gastronomic Terms",
page 53

**agrio** sour; bitter

**agua** water; **aguardiente**
brandy; **agua con gas**
sparkling mineral water;
**agua mineral** mineral
water

**ahumado** smoked

**aire** air; **aire
acondicionado** air-
conditioning

**aire libre, al** outside

**ajo** garlic

**albahaca** basil

**albaricoque** apricot

**Albariño** see "Wines", page
23

**albóndigas** meatballs, see
"The Basics", page 27

**alcachofa** artichoke

**alcachofas rellenas** stuffed
artichokes , see "National
Dishes", page 28

**alcaparras** capers

**alcohólico** alcoholic

**alcublas** see "Wines", page
23

**alemán** German

**Alemania** Germany

**alergia** allergy

**algo** something; anything

**algodón** cotton

**alguien** someone;
somebody; anybody

**algún** some; someone

**algunos** some; a few (pl)

**Alicante** see "Cheeses", page 8

**ali-oli** see "Gastronomic Terms", page 53

**almidón** starch

**alimentación** nutrition; diet

**almeja** clam, see "Seafood", page 17; **almejas a la marinera** clam marinara, see "National Dishes", page 28 and "Recipes", page 57; **almejas guisadas** see "National Dishes", page 28

**almendras** almonds

**almendras garrapiñadas** see "Sweets, Cakes, and Pastries", page 20

**al menos** at least

**almíbar en** see "Gastronomic Terms", page 55

**almohada / almohadilla** cushion; pillow

**alquiler** rent; hire

**alrededores** neighborhood; surroundings

**alubias** beans

**amargo** bitter

**amarillo** yellow

**a menudo** often

**amigo** friend

**anchoa** anchovy

**andoya** see "Cold Cut Meats", page 13

**anguila** eel; **anguilas al horno** baked eel, see "National Dishes", page 28; **anguilas con guisantes** eel and peas, see "National Dishes", page 28

**angulas a la cazuela**, see "Regional Dishes", page 39; **angulas a la vasca** Basque-style eel fries, see "Regional Dishes", page 48

**ángulo** angle

**anís** anise; aniseed

**antes** before

**antibiótico** antibiotic

**año** year

**apagar** to turn off; to put out

**aparcamiento** car park; parking lot

**apellido** surname

**aperitivo** aperitif

**apetito** appetite

**apio** celery

**aquí** here

**arenque** herring

**Armada** see "Cheeses", page 8

**aroma** aroma; fragrance
**aromático** aromatic
**arroz** rice; **arroz a la zamorana** see "Regional Dishes", page 42; **arroz amb fesols y naps**, see "Regional Dishes", page 51; **arroz blanco** white rice, see "National Dishes", page 28; **arroz con almejas** rice and clams, see "National Dishes", page 29; **arroz con costra** see "Regional Dishes", page 51; **arroz con leche** see "Sweets, Cakes, and Pastries", page 20; **arroz con riñones** rice and kidneys, see "National Dishes", page 29
**asado** roast
**asador** spit
**asaduras** entrails; offal; giblets
**ascensor** lift
**áspero** sour; bitter
**aspirina** aspirin
**atento** attentive; alert
**atún** tuna; **atún asado** baked tuna, see "National Dishes", page 29; **atún con tomate** tuna and tomato, see "National Dishes", page 29

**Austria** Austria
**austríaco** Austrian
**auténtico** authentic; genuine; original
**autobús** bus
**avellanas** hazelnuts
**avión** airplane
**ayer** yesterday
**ayudar** to help
**azafrán** saffron
**azúcar** sugar
**azucarero** sugar bowl

**bacalao** dried salted cod; **bacalao al pil pil**, see "Regional Dishes", page 48; **bacalao a la vizcaína** see "Regional Dishes", page 48; **bacalao al horno** baked dried salted cod, see "National Dishes", page 29
**bailar** to dance
**banco** bank
**bandeja** tray
**baño** toilet, bathroom
**bar** bar; café
**barato** economical; cheap; inexpensive
**Barcelona** Barcelona
**bastar** to be sufficient; to be enough
**batido** (milk) shake

**batir** to beat; to whip up; to whisk

**beber** to drink

**bebida** drink

**bechamel** see "The Basics", page 27

**berberecho** see "Seafood", page 17

**berenjena** eggplant

**berza** cabbage

**besugo** sea bream; **besugo al horno** baked sea bream, see "National Dishes", page 29; **besugo a la madrileña** Madrid-style sea bream. see "Regional Dishes", page 43

**Betanzos** see "Wines", page 23

**Beyos, queso de los** see "Cheeses", page 11

**bien** well; good

**bienvenido** welcome

**Bierzo** see "Wines", page 23

**bígaro** see "Seafood", page 17

**billete** ticket

**biscotes** biscuits

**bistec a la plancha** grilled steak

**bizcochos** see "Sweets, Cakes, and Pastries", page 20

**blanco** white

**blando** tender

**blancos** see "Cold Cut Meats", page 13

**blanquet** see "Cold Cut Meats", page 13

**boca** mouth

**bocadillo** (filled) roll, see "Gastronomic Terms", page 54

**bodega** (wine) cellar

**bolígrafo** pen

**Boloña** Bologna

**bolso** bag

**bonito** beautiful; handsome

**botella** bottle

**botelo** see "Cold Cut Meats", page 13

**borlas** flakes

**botón** button

**bovino** bovine, beef

**brasa** coals; cinders; embers

**brazo** arm; **brazo de gitano** see "Sweets, Cakes, and Pastries", page 20

**brindis** toast

**bueno** good

**buey** ox; beef **buey de mar** see "Seafood", page 17

**buñuelos** fritters, see "Sweets, Cakes, and Pastries", page 20;

**buñuelos de manzanas** see "Regional Dishes" page 51;
**Burgos** see "Cheeses", page 8
**burrida de ratjada** see "Regional Dishes", page 40
**butifarra** see "Cold Cut Meats", page 14

**caballa** mackerel
**cabra** goat
**cabrales** see "Cheeses", page 9
**cabrito asado** see "National Dishes", page 29
**cacahuete** peanut
**cacao** cocoa
**cachuela extremeña** see "Regional Dishes" page 43
**cada** each; every
**caerse** to fall
**café** coffee; **café cortado** white coffee; **café con leche** cappuccino; **café descafeinado** decaffeinated; **café solo** black coffee
**caja** cash desk; checkout
**cajera** cashier
**calabacines** zucchini
**calabaza** pumpkin; gourd; marrow

**calamares** squid; **calamares a la romana** see "National Dishes", page 29; **calamares en su tinta** squid, see "National Dishes", page 30
**caldeirada de pescado** see "Regional Dishes" page 46
**caldereta asturiana** see "Regional Dishes" page 39; **caldereta de Cordero** see "Regional Dishes" page 42; **caldereta de langosta** see "Regional Dishes" page 40; **caldereta extremeña** see "Regional Dishes" page 43
**caldo** broth; soup; **caldo gallego** Galician broth, see "Regional Dishes" page 46, and "Recipes", page 58
**calefacción** heating
**calentar** to heat; to warm
**caliente** hot
**calle** street; road
**callos** tripe, see "National Dishes", page 30 and "Recipes", page 59; **callos a la madrileña** see "Regional Dishes" page 44
**calmante** sedative
**calorías** calories
**camarero/a** waiter/waitress
**cambiar** to change

**cambio** exchange rate
**caminar** to walk
**camisa** shirt
**camomila** camomile
**campesina, a la** see "Gastronomic Terms", page 53
**campo** field; countryside
**canapés** see "Other Specialties", page 25
**canción** song
**canelones** cannelloni, see "National Dishes", page 30
**cangrejo** crab; **cangrejo de mar** see "Seafood", page 17; **cangrejos de río** river crabs, see "Regional Dishes" page 43
**caracoles** snails; **caracoles pagesos** see "Regional Dishes" page 40; **caracoles a la riojana** see "Regional Dishes" page 49
**caramelo** caramel; sweet; candy
**cardos** cardoon
**cargar en cuenta** to debit; to charge
**carne** meat; **carne a trozos** stew; **carne de cerdo con leche** see "Regional Dishes", page 40; **carne en lata** canned meat;

**carne mechada** see "National Dishes", page 30; **carne triturada** minced meat
**carnero** mutton; lamb
**carnet de identidad** identity card
**carnicería** butcher
**caro** expensive; dear
**cartera** wallet
**casa** house; **de la casa** see "Gastronomic Terms", page 54
**cáscara** door
**casero** homemade
**casi** almost
**castaña** chestnut
**catar** to taste; to try
**Cava** see "Wines", page 23
**caviar** caviar
**caza** game; hunting
**cazuela** (cooking) pot; saucepan; **a la cazuela** see "Gastronomic Terms", page 53
**cebolla** onion
**cedro** citron
**cecina** see "Cold Cut Meats", page 14
**cena** dinner
**cenicero** ashtray
**ceniza** ash

**centollo** see "Seafood", page 18

**central** central

**centro** centre

**cepillo** brush

**cerdo** pig; pork

**cerebro** brain

**cerebro** see "Cheeses", page 9

**cerezas** cherries

**cerilla** match

**cerrado** closed

**cerrar** to close

**cerveza** beer; **c. clara** lager; **c. de barril** draught; **c. grande** large; **c. oscura** stout; **c. pequeña** small

**ciento** hundred

**cierre** closure

**cigala** see "Seafood", page 18

**cigarrillo** cigarette

**cigarro** cigar

**ciruelas** plum

**cita** appointment; date

**ciudad** city

**clara de huevo** eggwhite

**claro** clear; pale

**cliente** client; customer

**coca** see "Regional Dishes" page 40

**cocer** to cook

**cocido** boiled; cooked **cocido madrileño** see "National Dishes", page 30; "Recipes", page 60; "Regional Dishes", page 44

**cocinero** cook

**cocción** cooking; baking

**coco** coconut

**coche** automobile; car

**cochecito de niños** pram; baby carriage

**cochifrito** see "Regional Dishes" page 49

**cochinillo** piglet **cochinillo asado** roast piglet, see "Regional Dishes", page 43; see "National Dishes", page 30

**codorniz** quail; **codorniz en su salsa** see "National Dishes", page 31

**coger** to take

**coliflor** cauliflower; **coliflor frita** fried cauliflower, see "National Dishes", page 31

**color** color

**colorantes** coloring agents

**comenzar** to start; to begin

**comer** to eat

**comida** lunch

**como** how; like; as; such as

**cómodo** convenient; comfortable

**compota de manzana** see "National Dishes", page 31

**compra** expense; **ir de compras** to go shopping

**comprar** to buy

**comprendido** included; inclusive

**comunicación** communication; announcement; message

**con** with

**concha** shell

**conejo** rabbit, see "National Dishes", page 31; **conejo con peras** rabbit and pears, see "Regional Dishes" page 45

**con gas** fizzy

**congrio** conger; **congrio con almejas** conger eel and clam, see "National Dishes", page 31

**con hielo** with ice

**con mantequilla** buttered; with butter

**confeccionado** packaged; wrapped-up; ready-made

**confeti** sugar-coated almonds

**confirmar** to confirm

**congelado** frozen

**conservantes** preservatives

**contado, al** in cash

**contento** happy; content

**continuar** to continue

**contra** against

**controlar** to control; to check

**copa** dish; tub

**corbata** tie

**cordero** spring lamb; **cordero en chilindrón** see "Regional Dishes" page 48

**corposo** full-bodied; thick; dense

**corriente** power supply; current

**cortado** cut; chopped

**cortar** to cut

**cosa** thing

**costar** to cost

**coste** cost

**costilla** cutlet; chop

**crema catalana** see "Sweets, Cakes, and Pastries", page 20

**crianza** breeding; farming (of animals)

**cristal** glass; crystal

**croissant** croissant

**croqueta** croquette

**crudeza** raw vegetables

**crudo** raw; uncooked
**crujiente** crisp; crunchy
**crustáceos** shellfish
**cual** what; which; which one
**cualquiera** any; whatever
**cuando** when
**cuanto** how much; how many
**cuarto** fourth; quarter
**cubiertos** cutlery
**cubito** ice-cube
**cubrir** to cover
**cuchara** spoon
**cucharilla** teaspoon
**cuchillo** knife
**cuenta** bill; account
**cuidar** to keep; to guard
**cuinat** see "Regional Dishes" page 41

**champán** champagne
**chanfaina** see "National Dishes", page 31 and "Regional Dishes", page 37
**chaqueta** jacket
**cheque** check; cheque
**Cheste** see "Wines", page 23
**chico/a** boy/girl
**chipirones en su tinta** see "Regional Dishes" page 48;

**chipirones fritos** see "National Dishes", page 31; **chipirones rellenos** see "Regional Dishes" page 48
**chirlas** small clams, see "Seafood", page 18
**chistorra** see "Cold Cut Meats", page 14
**chocolate** chocolate
**chorizo** red salami, see "Cold Cut Meats", page 14
**chuleta** chop; **chuletas/chuletillas de cordero** spring-lamb cutlets, see "National Dishes", page 31; **chuletas a la aragonesa** see "Regional Dishes" page 50
**chuletón** giant steak, see "National Dishes", page 31
**Chulilla** see "Wines", page 23
**chupete** dummy; pacifier
**churrasco** grilled meat
**churros** see "Sweets, Cakes, and Pastries", page 20

**dar** to give
**dar vueltas** to turn
**dátiles** dates
**debajo** under
**deber** to have to; must

**débil** weak

**decir** to say

**decoración** decoration

**decorado** decorated

**degustación** taste; tasting

**degustar** to taste; to enjoy

**dejar** to leave; to stop

**delgado** thin; lean

**demasiado** too much; too

**de nada** don't mention it!; you're welcome!

**dentadura postiza** dentures; set of false teeth

**dentón** dentex (fish)

**dentro (de)** in; inside

**depositar** to deposit

**derecha** right

**desinfectante** disinfectant

**desinfectar** to disinfect

**después** after; then

**destapar** to uncork

**desvanecido** fainted

**detrás** behind

**día** day

**diabético** diabetic

**diario** weekday

**diciembre** December

**dieta** diet

**difícil** difficult

**diga** Hello? (telephone)

**digerible** digestible

**digestivo** digestive

**dinero** silver

**dinero suelto** (small) change

**dirección** address

**director** manager; director

**discoteca** discothéque; disco

**distancia** distance

**distinto** different

**distribuidor** distributor; vending machine

**divisa** currency

**doble** double

**documento** document

**dólares** dollars

**dolor** pain

**dolor de barriga** bellyache; **dolor de estómago** stomachache; **dolor de cabeza** headache

**domingo** Sunday

**donde** where

**dorada** gilthead bream; **dorada a la sal** see "Regional Dishes", page 51

**dorado** browned; golden brown

**dulce** sweet; mild

**dulces** sweets; candies; confectionery

**dulcificante** sweetener

**duro** hard

**embajada** embassy

**embarazada** pregnant

**embutidos** sausages; cold cut meats; **embutidos mixtos** see "National Dishes", page 32

**empanada** see "Other Specialties", page 25; **empanada gallega** see "Regional Dishes" page 46

**empanadas** see "Regional Dishes" page 41

**empanadilla** see "Other Specialties", page 25

**empanado** breaded

**emparedados** canapé

**en aceite** in oil

**en cambio** instead (of)

**encéfalo** brain

**encender** to light; to turn on

**encendido** lit; on

**encima** on; above

**endivia** endive

**enfermar** to fall ill; to be taken ill

**enfermo** ill; sick

**enfriar** to cool

**ensaimadas** see "Sweets, Cakes, and Pastries", page 21; see "Regional Dishes" page 41

**ensalada** salad

**ensaladilla rusa** Russian salad, see "National Dishes", page 32

**en seguida** at once; straight away

**entender** to understand

**entero** whole

**entrada** entry; entrance

**entrar** to enter

**entre** amongst; within; between

**entrecote de ternera** see "National Dishes", page 32

**entremés** hors-d'oeuvres; appetizer

**en vinagre** pickled

**equivocación** mistake

**error** error

**escabechada** marinade

**escabeche** pickled in vinegar, see "Gastronomic Terms", page 55

**escaldón canario** see "Regional Dishes" page 41

**escaleras** stairs

**escalivada** see "Regional Dishes" page 45

**escalopes** breaded minute steaks, see "The Basics", page 27

**escribir** to write

**escudella** see "Regional Dishes" page 45

**España** Spain

**español** Spanish

**espárragos** asparagus, see "National Dishes", page 32

**especias** spices; aromatic herbs

**espectáculo** show; performance

**esperar** to hope; to wait

**espinacas** spinach

**estación** station; season

**Estados Unidos** United States

**estanco** tobacconist's

**esta noche** this evening

**este** this

**estofado** stew; **estofado a la asturiana** see "Regional Dishes", page 39; **estofado de buey** beef stew, see "Regional Dishes", page 39

**estrecho** narrow; tight

**estropeado** broken; out of order; (mechanical) failure

**estudiar** to study

**evitar** to avoid

**excepto** except

**excursión** excursion; trip

**experto** expert

**exposición** exhibition

**externo** external; outside

**extranjero** foreign; foreigner; overseas

**fabada asturiana** see "Regional Dishes" page 39 and "Recipes", page 61

**fabes con almejes** see "Regional Dishes" page 39

**fácil** easy

**factura** invoice

**faisán** pheasant

**familia** family

**familiar** familiar; family (adj)

**famoso** famous

**farmacéutico** chemist; pharmacist

**fariñón** see "Cold Cut Meats" page 14

**farmacia** chemist's; pharmacy; drugstore

**favor, por** please

**febrero** February

**feo** bad; ugly

**fiambre** mixed sausages, see "Gastronomic Terms", page 55

**fideos** noodles

**fideua** see "Regional Dishes" page 51

**fiesta** party; fête; public holiday

**filete (de carne)** minute steak, see "The Basics", page 27

**filetes** fillets

**filetes de ternera** see "National Dishes", page 32

**filetes empanados** breaded minute steaks, see "National Dishes", page 32

**filtrar** to filter

**filloas** see "Regional Dishes" page 46

**fin** end

**firma** signature

**flan** see "Sweets, Cakes, and Pastries", page 21

**flaó** see "Regional Dishes" page 41

**flores** flowers

**floristería** florist

**fotografía** photograph

**francés** French

**Francia** France

**freír** to fry

**fresa** strawberry

**fresco** fresh, cool

**fresones** raspberries

**frigorífico** refrigerator

**frío** cold

**frito** fried

**fritura** frying; fried food; fry; fry-up

**frixuelos** see "Regional Dishes" page 39

**fruta** fruit

**frutos selváticos** wild berries

**fuego** fire

**fuera** outside

**fuet** see "Cold Cut Meats", page 15

**fumador** smoker

**funcionar** to work; to function; to run; to operate

**gallina** hen; **gallina en pepitoria** see "Regional Dishes", page 48

**gallo** cock

**gallo capado** capon

**gallo pequeño** cockerel; young cock

**gambas** prawns, see "Seafood", page 18

**gamonedo** see "Cheeses", page 9

**garbanzos** chick-peas

**garganta** throat

**garrafa** carafe; jug; decanter

**gazpacho andaluz** see "Regional Dishes" page 38

**gelatina** gelatin; jelly

**género** kind; sort; type; gender

**Génova** Genoa

**gorbea** see "Cheeses", page 9

**gordo** fat

**gracias** thank you

**Gran Bretaña** Great Britain

**grande** big; large; great

**granizado** water ice

**graso** fat

**gratén, al** see "Gastronomic Terms", page 53

**gratinado** (au) gratin

**gratinado de berenjenas** aubergines au gratin see "National Dishes", page 32 and "Regional Dishes", page 44

**gratis** for free; for nothing; without charge

**grosella** blackcurrant

**grupo** group

**guantes** gloves

**guarda** caretaker; guardian; keeper

**guardarropa** cloakroom

**guarnición** vegetables; side dish

**guía** guide

**guía telefónica** phone book

**guinda** sour cherry drink; sour (black) cherry

**guindilla** hot pepper; chili pepper

**guisado de trigo** see "Regional Dishes", page 51

**guisantes** peas

**guiso** gravy

**guiso de caracoles** see "Regional Dishes" page 38

**guiso de rabo de toro** see "Regional Dishes", page 38

**gusto** taste; flavor

**habas** broad beans

**habitación** room

**hacer** to do; to make

**hambre** hunger

**harina** flour

**Haro** see "Wines", page 23

**hasta** until; as far as

**heladería** ice-cream shop

**helado** ice-cream, see "Sweets, Cakes, and Pastries", page 21

**hervir** to boil

**hielo** ice

**hierbas, a las** see "Gastronomic Terms", page 53

**higadillos** chicken liver

**hígado** liver

**hijo** son
**hilo** thread; line; wire
**hinojo** fennel; **hinojos con jamón** fennel and ham, see "Regional Dishes", page 50
**hoja** leaf, sheet of paper
**hojaldre** cream puff
**Holanda** Holland
**hombre** man
**hombro** shoulder
**homogeneizado** homogenized; baby food
**hora** hour
**hora, a la** on time
**horario** timetable; schedule
**horno** oven; **al horno** see "Gastronomic Terms", page 53
**hortalizas** vegetables
**hospital** hospital
**hotel** hotel
**hueso** bone
**huevos** eggs; **h. al plato** see "National Dishes", page 32; **h. a la flamenca** see "Regional Dishes", page 38; **h. con mantequilla** eggs fried in butter; **h. duros** hard-boiled eggs; **h. revueltos** scrambled eggs

**humeante** smoking; steaming
**humo** smoke

**idiazábal** see "Cheeses", page 10
**igual** equal
**impermeable** waterproof; raincoat
**importancia, a la** see "Gastronomic Terms", page 53
**importante** important
**imposible** impossible
**incluido** included
**incómodo** uncomfortable; awkward; inconvenient
**indicaciones** directions; indications
**información** information
**informar** informer
**Inglaterra** England
**inglés** English
**inicio** start; beginning
**inocuo** harmless; inoffensive
**insecto** insect
**integral** total; complete; wholemeal; integral
**interior** internal; interior
**interno** internal; inside; (telephone) extension

**interurbana** long-distance call

**intoxicación** poisoning; intoxication

**invierno** winter

**invitar** to invite

**ir** to go

**Irlanda** Ireland

**irse** to leave; to depart

**Italia** Italy

**italiano** Italian

**jabón** soap

**jamón** ham, see "Cold Cut Meats", page 15; **jamón con guisantes** ham and peas, see "National Dishes", page 32

**jarabe** syrup

**jardín** garden

**jardinera, a la** see "Gastronomic Terms", page 54

**jarra** jug

**jefe** chef , chief

**Jerez** see "Wines", page 23; **al Jerez** see "Gastronomic Terms", page 54

**joven** young

**judías con chorizo** see "Regional Dishes", page 50

**judías verdes** French beans, see "National Dishes", page 33

**judiones** broad beans; **judiones de la granja** see "Regional Dishes", page 43

**juego** game

**jueves** Thursday

**jugar** to play

**julio** July

**Jumilla** see "Wines", page 24

**junio** June

**juntar** to join; to gather; to put together

**junto a** beside; next to

**kaki** persimmon

**kiwi** kiwi fruit

**lacón** see "Cold Cut Meats", page 15; **lacón con grelos** see "Regional Dishes", page 46

**lago** lake

**langosta** lobster, see "Seafood", page 18

**langostino** baby lobster, see "Seafood", page 18; see "National Dishes", page 33

**lápiz** pencil

**largo** long

**las mijas** see "Regional Dishes", page 44

**lata** tin; can

**laurel** bay leaf

**lavar** to wash

**Lebeña, quesucos de** see "Cheeses", page 11

**lechazo castellano** see "Regional Dishes", page 43

**leche** milk

**lechuga** lettuce

**leer** to read

**legumbres** legumes

**lejos** far

**lengua** tongue

**lenguado** sole; **lenguado al horno** baked sole, see "National Dishes", page 33

**lenguas de gato** see "Sweets, Cakes, and Pastries", page 21

**lente** lens

**lentejas** lentils; **lentejas al estilo de Burgos** see "Regional Dishes", page 44; **lentejas con sobrasada** see "Regional Dishes", page 41

**lentillas** contact lenses

**León** see "Cheeses", page 10

**levadura** yeast

**libre** free; clear; vacant

**libro** book

**licor** liqueur

**liebre** hare

**ligero** light

**limón** lemon

**limpiar** to clean

**limpio** clean

**línea** line

**liso** smooth; straight

**lista** list

**listo** ready

**litro** liter

**local** local; room; place; premises; bar

**lomo embuchado**, loin, see "Cold Cut Meats", page 15

**longaniza** see "Cold Cut Meats", page 15

**Los Oteros** see "Wines", page 24

**lubina** bass; **lubina asada** oven-baked sea bass, see "National Dishes", page 33

**lucio** pike

**lugar** place

**lunes** Monday

**luz** light

**llama** flame

**llamada telefónica** phone call

**llamar** to call; to phone
**llegar** to arrive
**lleno** full
**lleno de gente** crowded
**llevar** to bring; to carry; to wear

**macedonia** fruit salad
**macrobiótico** macrobiotic
**madre** mother
**Madrid** Madrid
**maduro** ripe; mature
**maíz** maize; corn
**mal/o** bad; evil
**malentendido** misunderstanding
**maleta** suitcase
**mañana** morning; tomorrow; tomorrow morning
**mandarina** tangerine
**manjar** dish; (main) course
**mano** hand
**manteca** lard
**mantel** tablecloth
**mantequilla** butter
**manzana** apple; **manzanas al horno** see "Sweets, Cakes, and Pastries", page 21; **manzanas rellenas de nuez y cocco** see "National Dishes", page 33

**mar** sea
**marido** husband
**marinera, a la** see "Gastronomic Terms", page 54
**mariscos** seafood
**marrones** chestnuts
**martes** Tuesday
**marzo** March
**más** more
**masticar** to chew; to masticate
**mayo** May
**mayonesa** mayonnaise
**medicina** medicine
**médico** doctor
**medio** half; means
**mejor** better; best
**mejillones** mussels, see "Seafood" page 18; **mejillones al vapor** steamed mussels, see "National Dishes", page 33; **mejillones al vino blanco** mussels in white wine sauce, see "Regional Dishes", page 47
**melocotón** peach
**melón** melon
**menestra** soup, see "National Dishes", page 33
**menos** less; minus

**menta** mint
**menú** menu
**mercado** market
**merienda** snack
**merluza** hake; **merluza a la cazuela** hake casserole, see "National Dishes", page 33 and "Recipes", page 63; **merluza a la sidra** cidered hake, see "Regional Dishes", page 40; **merluza a la vasca** see "Regional Dishes", page 49
**mermelada** jam
**mes** month
**mesa** table
**metro** subway
**mezcla** blend; mixture
**mezclar** to mix; to blend
**miel** honey
**mientras** while; whereas
**miércoles** Wednesday
**migas** see "Other Specialties", page 25
**mil** thousand
**milhojas** see "National Dishes", page 33
**minusválido** disabled
**minuto** minute
**mirar** to watch; to look at
**mitad** half

**mismo** same; self
**mixto** mix; mixed
**modo** way; manner
**molestar** to disturb
**mollejas** sweetbread
**moluscos** molluscs; shellfish
**moneda** coin
**Monterrey** see "Wines", page 24
**Montilla** see "Wines", page 24
**Montroy** see "Wines", page 24
**monumentos** monuments
**morcilla** see "National Dishes", page 33; see "Cold Cut Meats", page 15
**morcón** see "Cold Cut Meats", page 15
**morros de ternera a la asturiana** see "Regional Dishes", page 40
**morteruelo** see "Regional Dishes", page 44
**mosca** fly
**mosquitos** mosquito; gnat
**mostaza** mustard
**mostrar** to show
**mucho** a lot; much; very
**mujer** woman; wife
**muro** wall
**museo** museum

**música** music
**muslo** thigh
**muy** many, very

**nada** nothing
**nadar** to swim
**nadie** no; nobody; none
**naranja** orange; **naranjada** orangeade
**nata** cream; **nata con nueces** see "National Dishes", page 34; **nata líquida** single cream; **nata montada** whipped cream
**natillas** flan, see "Sweets, Cakes, and Pastries", page 21
**natural, al** see "Gastronomic Terms", page 54
**Navidad** Christmas
**necesidad** need
**necesitar** to have need of
**nécora** see "Seafood", page 19
**negro** black
**ningún/o** no one; nobody
**no fumador** non-smoking
**noche** night
**Nochebuena** Christmas Eve
**Nochevieja** New Year's Eve
**nombre** name

**norte** north
**noviembre** November
**novillo** beef
**nueces** walnuts
**nuez moscada** nutmeg
**número** number
**nunca** never

**obligar** to oblige; to force; to compel
**obligatorio** compulsory; obligatory
**obtener** to obtain
**oca** goose
**octubre** October
**ocupado** busy; engaged; taken
**oír** to hear; to feel
**ojo** eye
**olor** smell; odor
**olvidar** to forget
**olla gitana** see "Regional Dishes", page 38; **olla podrida** see "Regional Dishes", page 50
**ordenar** to order
**orduña** see "Cheeses", page 10
**orégano** oregano; marjoram
**oro** gold
**oscuro** dark

**ostra** oyster, see "Seafood", page 19

**otro** other

**padre** father

**padres** parents

**paella** see "National Dishes", page 34; **paella valenciana** see "Recipes", page 63 and see "Regional Dishes", page 52

**pagar** to pay

**pago** payment

**país** country; land; village; town

**palabra** word

**palillo** toothpick; wooden skewer

**paloma** dove

**pan** bread

**pan de molde** loaf of bread

**pan rallado** breadcrumbs

**pandilla** party; group; company

**pañuelo** handkerchief; **pañuelo de papel** paper tissue

**papel** paper

**par** pair

**para** for; per; in order to

**parada** stop

**paraguas** umbrella

**parar** to stop

**parrilla** grill; **a la parrilla** see "Gastronomic Terms", page 54

**parque** park

**parte** part

**pasaporte** passport

**pasiego** see "Cheeses", page 10

**pasta** pasta

**pastel** tart; cake; pie; **pastel de la abuela** see "Sweets, Cakes, and Pastries", page 21

**pastelería** cakeshop

**pastillas** pill; **pastiglia de avecrem** stock (bouillon) cube

**patatas** potatoes; **patatas a la riojana** see "Regional Dishes", page 50; **patatas asadas** roast potatoes; **patatas cocidas** boiled potatoes; **patatas con carne** meat and potatoes, see "National Dishes", page 34; **patatas fritas** chips; French fries

**pato** duck; **pato al horno** Roast duck, see "National Dishes", page 34

**pavo** turkey

**pecho** breast; chest

**pechugas de pollo** see "National Dishes", page 34

**pedir** to ask

**pelar** to pluck; to peel

**pencas de acelga gratinada** see "Regional Dishes", page 50

**pendientes** earrings

**pepinos** cucumbers

**pequeño** small

**pera** pear

**perca** perch

**percebe** see "Seafood", page 19

**perder** to lose

**perdices con chocolate** see "Regional Dishes", page 49

**perdiz** partridge; **perdiz estofada** see "Regional Dishes", page 44

**perejil** parsley

**periódico** newspaper

**permitido** permission; permit

**permitir** to permit; to allow

**pescadilla** whiting

**pescado** fish

**pestiños** see "Regional Dishes", page 52

**petición** request; demand

**picadillo** see "National Dishes", page 34

**picante** hot; spicy

**pichón** pigeon

**picón de Tresviso** see "Cheeses", page 10

**pie** foot

**pierna** leg

**píldora** pill

**pimentón** hot and mild red bell pepper powder

**pimienta** pepper

**pimiento** bell pepper; **pimientos rellenos** stuffed bell peppers, see "National Dishes", page 34

**pinchos** see "Gastronomic Terms", page 55

**pincho moruno** see "National Dishes", page 34

**piñones** pine nuts

**piscina** swimming pool

**pistachos** pistachio nuts

**pisto manchego** see "Regional Dishes", page 44

**placer** to please

**plátano** banana

**plato** dish; course; plate

**plato, al** see "Gastronomic Terms", page 54

**plato combinado** see "Gastronomic Terms", page 55

**plaza** square

**pochas a la Navarra** see "Regional Dishes", page 50

**poco** little; not much; a few

**poder** to be able, can

**pollo** chicken; **pollo al chilindrón** see "Regional Dishes", page 50; **pollo al Jerez** see "Regional Dishes", page 38; **pollo asado** see "National Dishes", page 35; **pollo campurriano** see "Regional Dishes", page 40

**polo** popsicle

**polvorones** see "Sweets, Cakes, and Pastries", page 21

**polvos de talco** talcum powder

**pomelo** grapefruit

**poner** to put; to place

**poner la mesa** to lay the table

**por** for; per

**porción** portion

**porque** why; because

**posible** possible

**postal** postcard

**postre** dessert

**precio** price

**preferir** to prefer

**preguntar** question

**preparar** to prepare

**prisa** hurry; haste

**probar** to taste

**propina** tip

**propio** just; really; own

**puchero canario** see "Regional Dishes", page 42

**pueblo** country; village; people

**puerros** leeks

**puerta** door

**pulpa** pulp; flesh

**pulpo** octopus; **pulpo afeira** see "Regional Dishes", page 47; **pulpo a la gallega**, see "National Dishes", page 35

**puntas** honey mushrooms

**puré** purée, see "The Basics", page 27

**puro** cigar

**purrusalda** see "Regional Dishes", page 49

**puzol** see "Cheeses", page 11

**que** that

**¡qué aproveche!** Have a good meal!

**quedar/se** to stay; to remain; to be left

**quemado** burnt

**quemar** to burn

**querer** to want

**queso** cheese

**queso de los Beyos** see "Cheeses", page 11

**quesucos de Lebeña** see "Cheeses", page 11

**quien** who

**quitar** to remove

**quitar la monda** to peel; **quitar la grasa** to scour; to remove the grease from; **quitar la cáscara** to shell

**quizás** perhaps

**rábanos** radishes

**ración** portion

**radio** radio

**rallado** grated

**rape** angler fish, goosefish, monkfish; **rape a la gallega** see "Regional Dishes", page 47

**rápidamente** quickly

**rápido** rapid; quick; fast

**rebado de Cáceres** see "Regional Dishes", page 44

**recao de Binéfar** see "Regional Dishes", page 50

**receta** recipe

**recibir** to receive

**recibo** receipt

**reclamación** complaint

**reembolso** refund

**región** region

**regresar** to return

**regreso** return

**reloj** watch, clock

**relleno** stuffing; filling; stuffed; filled, see "Gastronomic Terms", page 55

**remolacha** beetroot; beet

**reo con almejas** sea trout and clams, see "Regional Dishes", page 47

**repollo** cabbage

**reservado** reserved; booked

**reservar** to reserve; to book

**responder** to reply; to answer; to respond

**restaurante** restaurant

**resto** change

**retraso** delay

**retraso, con** late

**revuelto** see "Gastronomic Terms", page 56; **revuelto de gambas y ajetes** see "National Dishes", page 35

**Ribeiro** see "Wines", page 24

**riñón** kidney

**riñones al Jerez** see "Regional Dishes", page 38

**róbalo** grey mullet

**rodajas, en** see "Gastronomic Terms", page 55

**rojo** red

**rollos** roulades, see "The Basics" page 27

**rollos de ternera** veal roulades, see "National Dishes", page 35

**romero** rosemary

**romper** to break

**Rosal** see "Wines", page 24

**rosca/ón** or **rosquilla** ring-shaped cake; donut

**roto** broken

**Rueda** see "Wines", page 24

**ruido** noise

**ruidoso** noisy

**rústico** country-style

**sábado** Saturday

**saber** to know

**sabor** flavor; taste

**saborear** to taste; to enjoy; to season

**sabroso** tasty

**sal** salt

**sala** hall; lounge; room

**salado** salty; salted; savory

**salar** to salt; to add salt to

**salchicha** sausage, see "Cold Cut Meats", page 16

**salchichón** see "Cold Cut Meats", page 16

**salero** salt-cellar

**salida** exit

**salir** to go out; to come out; to leave

**salmón** salmon; **salmón ahumado** smoked salmon; **salmón a noso estilo** see "Regional Dishes", page 47; **salmón asado** baked salmon, see "National Dishes", page 35

**salmonetes** red mullet

**salpicón de Murcia** see "Regional Dishes", page 52

**salsa** sauce; **salsa tártara** see "Gastronomic Terms", page 55; **salsa verde** see "Gastronomic Terms", page 55

**salvia** sage

**sancocho canario** see "Regional Dishes", page 42

**sandía** water-melon

**sangría** see "Other Specialties", page 25

**San Simón** see "Cheeses", page 11

**sardinas** sardines; **sardinas fritas** fried sardines, see "National Dishes", page 35

**sartén** frying pan; saucepan

**seco** dry

**sed** thirst

**segundo** second

**sello** stamp

**semana** week

**señora** lady; madam; Mrs

**señorita** young woman; Miss

**separado** separate

**sepias** cuttlefish

**septiembre** September

**servicio** service; service charge

**servilleta** serviette; napkin

**sesos** brains

**setas** mushrooms

**sidra** see "Other Specialties", page 25

**siempre** always; ever

**silla** chair

**silla para bebés** high chair

**simple** simple

**sin** without

**sin alcohol** non-alcoholic; alcohol-free

**sitio** place; position; job; seat

**sobrasada** see "Cold Cut Meats", page 16

**sobre** envelope

**sofrito** onion and herbs browned in oil

**soja** soya

**solo** alone

**sólo** only

**solomillo** see "National Dishes", page 35

**sombrero** hat; sombrero

**sopa** soup; **sopa castellana** see "Regional Dishes", page 43; **sopa del Teide** see "Regional Dishes", page 42; **sopa de puré** see "National Dishes", page 35; **sopa de ajo** see "National Dishes", page 35; **sopa seca mallorquina** see "Regional Dishes", page 41

**sorbete** sorbet; sherbet **sorbete de naranja** see "National Dishes", page 35

**soria** see "Cheeses", page 11

**subir** to go up; to climb; to mount; to get on; to raise

**suceder** to happen; to take place; to occur

**sucio** dirty

**suflé de patatas** see "National Dishes", page 36

**suido** pork; pig

**Suiza** Switzerland

**suquet de peix** see "Regional Dishes", page 45

**sur** south

**sutil** thin; fine; subtle

**tacita** coffee cup

**también** also

**tapa** lid

**tapas** snack

**tapón** cork; stopper; cap

**tarde** evening; late

**tarjeta de crédito** credit card

**tarrina** tureen

**tarta** tart; pie; cake **tarta de plátanos** see "Regional Dishes", page 42

**tasca** tavern; inn

**taza** cup

**té** tea

**teléfono** telephone

**temperatura** temperature

**tenedor** fork

**tener** to have; to hold; to keep

**tener que** to have to

**tentempié** appetizer

**terminar** to finish; to end

**ternero** veal

**terraza** terrace

**tetilla** see "Cheeses", page 11

**tiempo** weather; time

**tiempo, del** room temperature

**tienda** shop

**tinta, en su** see "Gastronomic Terms", page 55

**tirar** to throw away

**tirita** Band Aid

**tisana** herb tea

**toalla** towel

**tocinillos** see "Sweets, Cakes, and Pastries", page 22

**tocino** lard

**todavía** more; still; nevertheless

**todo** all; everything

**tombet de peix** see "Regional Dishes", page 41

**tomillo** thyme

**Toro** see "Wines", page 24

**torrijas** see "Sweets, Cakes, and Pastries", page 22

**torta**, see "Other Specialties", page 26

**torta con mermelada** jam tart

**torteta** see "Cold Cut Meats", page 16

**tortilla** omelette; **tortilla de ropa vieja** see "National

Dishes", page 36; **tortilla española** see "National Dishes", page 36 and "Recipes", page 65; **tortilla francesa** see "National Dishes", page 36; **tortilla paisana** see "National Dishes", page 36

**tostado** toasted

**trabajar** to work

**trabajo** work

**traer** to carry; to bring

**tranquilo** quiet; calm

**tren** train

**triturado** minced; chopped

**triturar** to mince; to chop

**trucha** trout; **truchas a la Navarra** see "Regional Dishes", page 50; **truchas al horno** baked trout, see "National Dishes", page 36; **truchas escabechadas** see "National Dishes", page 36

**Turín** Turin

**txangurro relleno** see "National Dishes", page 49

**último** last

**ulloa** see "Cheeses", page 11

**untado** greasy; oily

**usar** to use

**uvas** grapes

**uvas pasas** raisins

**vacaciones** holidays, vacation

**vacío** empty

**vainilla** vanilla

**Valdeorras** see "Wines", page 24

**valdeteja** see "Cheeses", page 12

**Valdevimbre** see "Wines", page 24

**vapor, al** see "Gastronomic Terms", page 54

**vaso** glass

**vegetariano** vegetarian see "Gastronomic Terms", page 56

**vela** candle

**vender** to sell

**venir** to come

**ventana** window

**ver** to see

**veraniego** summer (adj.)

**verano** summer

**verde** green

**verdura** vegetable

**vieira** see "Seafood", page 19

**vieiras con col** see "Regional Dishes", page 47

viejo old
viernes Friday
villalón see "Cheeses", page 12
vinagre vinegar
vinagreta, a la see see "Gastronomic Terms", page 54
vino wine; **v. blanco** white wine; **v. fuerte** full-bodied wine; **v. ligero** light wine; **v. rosado** rosé; **v. tinto** red wine
vista sight, view
vitaminas vitamins

volver to return; to go back; to come back
vuelo flight
vuelta tour; turn; trip; revolution

yema (huevo) egg yolk
yemas see "Sweets, Cakes, and Pastries", page 22
yoghurt yoghurt

zanahoria carrot
zumo juice
zumo natural freshly-squeezed fruit juice

# INDEX